good beach guide

the*beachgoer's* **Bible** to the **Ionian** *islands*

zakynthos

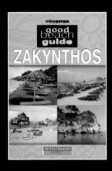

© Efstathiadis Group 2004

ISBN: 960-226-611-2

EFSTATHIADIS GROUP **S.A.**
88 Drakontos Str.,
104 42 Athens
tel.: ++3210 5154 650,
fax: ++3210 5154 657
e-mail: efgroup@otenet.gr
GREECE

Printed and bound in Greece

contents

aword**from**the**author** 5

usefulstuff** 6-15

all**greek**to**me 6

sea**turtles** 7

useful**websites** 10

european**blue**flag**beaches** 13

beach**grading**system 14

aboutzakynthos** 16-167

Introduction 20

generalinformation 21-25

history 21

culture 23

practicalinformation 26-31

island**travel** 26

resorts 32-46

beaches 47-167

ionian a to z 168-191

index 191
- a 170-171
- b 172-173
- c 173-175
- d 175-177
- e 177
- f 178-179
- i 179
- j 179
- m 179-180
- n 181
- o 181
- p 182-183
- r 183-185
- s 185-187
- t 187-189
- v 189-190
- w 190
- y 190

There are lots of excellent (and some not so excellent) guide books providing information about the mythology, history, culture and traditions of particular Greek Islands. Some even give a little current information about an island.

Very few, however, pay any attention to arguably the most important facet of your holiday - the beach. The Good Beach Guide has been produced to remedy that particular problem. Containing easy to read, invaluable information and pictures on a wide selection of beaches on each island, this is the beach-goers Bible when it comes to deciding where to lay your towel.

Beaches are included according to selection criteria such as geographical location and ease of access. A grading system helps to determine whether the beach is worth visiting. And if you want an isolated beach rather than an organised beach - the information is all immediately at hand, along with directions to get there and its proximity to main resorts.

Recognising that more and more visitors to Greece are choosing to make their own travel and accommodation arrangements, The Good Beach Guide also features detailed information on each of the main resorts, along with travel guidance and an A to Z of useful local information. It's the only «Lifestyle» guide of its type available in Greece.

When it comes to the beach... GREECE is the word

Mike Arran

aβc all GREEK to me

Greek is a phonetic language in which the way a word sounds is given considerably more prominence than the way it's spelled. Hence you will often see «lamp» on the menu instead of «lamb» or be offered «tzin» and tonic rather than «gin» and tonic. Whilst such eccentric spellings are a source of amusement to foreigners, they are a matter of pure logic to the average Greek who is simply spelling out the word as it seems to sound.

The situation is even more difficult for tourists when it comes to place names. It's nothing to see three or four different versions of the same place-name. Hence you may see Lagana, Lagenas or Lagena - in reality it will be the same place. More complicated are names that have a «foreign» version as well as a Greek one. So Corfu or Corfou will more frequently be expressed as Kerkyra! Cephalonia is also Kefalonia or Kefalinia. You just have to grin and bear it really!

Saints (whose names grace many, many locations) are also a nightmare as you'll see them expressed as male or female Agios or Agia (or Aghios, Ayios, Aghia or Ayia!) or shortened just to Ag. Plural saints will end in ii - Agii or similar. Confusing isn't it!

Most road maps are expressed bilingually with a Greek and English version of the names and it's always wisest to buy such a map. If you can't work out where you are from the map, stop and show it to a local. Chances are that they'll be able to direct you to your destination in English or, otherwise, draw you road directions.

It's always advisable to have at least two maps and you should buy the most recent ones you can. Comparison of the information contained on the two maps will normally get you to the desired location!

In this book, the normal Greek spelling of resorts and beaches is shown against the English version for each resort and beach. A «thumb-nail» map also identifies broadly where each place is located and you can compare this with the information contained on your own road map.

One final point; many names are so popular that there may well be more than one such location on a particular island. Check carefully that the Ag. Nikolaos or Agios Georgios you're heading to is the one you actually want to visit!

GREEK ALPHABET-PHONETIC PRONUNCIATION

α-Α	= alfa	ν-Ν	= ni
β-Β	= vita	ξ-Ξ	= xi
γ-Γ	= gama	ο-Ο	= omikron
δ-Δ	= delta	π-Π	= pi
ε-Ε	= epsilon	ρ-Ρ	= ro
ζ-Ζ	= zita	σ-Σ	= sigma
η-Η	= ita	τ-Τ	= taf
θ-Θ	= thita	υ-Υ	= ipsilon
ι-Ι	= giota	φ-Φ	= fi
κ-Κ	= kapa	χ-Χ	= xi
λ-Κ	= lamda	ψ-Ψ	= psi
μ-Μ	= mi	ω-Ω	= omega

SEA turtles

THE OLDEST TOURISTS ON IONIAN BEACHES!

Indian mythology suggests that the survival of the world depends on the continued existence of the sea turtle. As a prehistoric reptilian of some 200 million years duration, perhaps there is more truth in this myth than we would care to credit. With the exception of sea snakes, the sea turtle is the only reptilian associate of the dinosaurs to have made it through the centuries. How tragic if indiscriminate tourism is the catalyst of its extinction.

Caretta-Caretta (the «Loggerhead» sea turtle) breeds extensively on Zakynthos, Kefalonia and elsewhere within the Peloponnese. It makes use of warm, soft-sand beaches to continue its precarious existence. A male turtle will never return to land. Only the females come ashore - to dig nests and deposit eggs. Laying an average of 110 eggs on each occasion, they may return several times to nest during the breeding season. Adult females breed in this way every two or three years, returning to the beach of their own birth to continue the multi -million year life cycle.

7

Having laid her eggs, the incubation period of 45-60 days commences. The hatchlings then struggle to break out of their shells - a process which takes a few days. They are now at greatest risk. Not only do they face natural predators like dogs and gulls, they also have to contend with tourists!

The hatching process is initiated by a drop in temperature. Inadvertently spiking a nest with a sun umbrella can produce such a reduced temperature in the sand, resulting in premature evacuation and almost certain death for the hatchlings. This is why volunteers often place protective covers over nests on breeding beaches.

Normally, the cool night sand is the alarm bell which signals the babies to career en masse for the water. Their desperate, circular tracks in the sand can be daylight's only evidence of their brief existence. Misled by land-bound lights near to the beach, they career in the wrong direction, totally confused. By morning, sea birds will have greedily breakfasted on the youngsters. Enforced conservation measures, restricting development near certain breeding beaches is gradually changing this scenario.

Of course, the same beaches which delight the turtle also delight the tourist. Digging in the sand, driving a motor vehicle on the beach or inadvertently trampling on a nesting site - all can prematurely spur the youngsters into that seaward dash. Please assist by not driving any motor vehicle or riding motorbikes on the shore. Dig only close to the sea area, not in the softer, drier sand closer to dune areas. Flatten sand castles and fill holes prior to departure each day. Do not place the spikes of sun umbrellas into soft sand areas.

A number of trip boats on Zakynthos offer «guaranteed» sightings during the season. There is little that such activity can do to damage the turtles. Waiting and watching until one surfaces nearby is a harmless enough activity.

Those who like an early morning stroll along the beach may be lucky enough to see a turtle hatch and scuttle for the sea. However, most make their frantic escape for the water during the night hours when the moon is high. Equally, it is in the still of the night that the female drags her cumbersome frame onto the beach to deposit her eggs. At this point she «cries» - tears form in her eyes as a lubricant while she is in the hostile environment of land. This is why nesting beaches post notices imposing a curfew and tourists are required to avoid these areas at night.

The Sea Turtle Protection Society of Greece has been increasingly active over recent years. They have established observation points and protected nesting sites for the caretta-caretta. They also have information kiosks near nesting beaches and undertake informative slide shows and lectures in the nearby hotels. Tourists who want to do a little more can also become subscribing members of the Society. They also have major volunteer programmes that attract young people from all over Europe.

Some of the Society's scientists are actively engaged in monitoring nesting activities of the turtles. Only in this way can they assess whether the struggle to preserve the Loggerhead is succeeding. Tagging is undertaken to monitor development and movement and some Greek Loggerheads have turned up over 1500 km. away in Italy, Tunisia and Libya.

TEN GOLDEN RULES
TO PROTECT THE TURTLES

1 **Avoid** nesting beaches between sunset and sunrise.
2 **No** bright lights near beaches at night.
3 **No** cars or motorbikes on nesting beaches.
4 **Don't** put sun umbrellas in soft sand
5 **Take** your litter home with you.
6 **Knock down** sand castles and fill in holes before leaving.
7 **Don't** dig in soft sand areas.
8 **Don't** use speed boats near turtle beaches.
9 **Never** pick up a baby turtle to help it to the sea.
10 **Support** the protection of nesting areas from development.

The Sea Turtle Protection Society of Greece can be contacted

at: SOLOMOU 35, 10682 - ATHENS GREECE
Tel/fax: 0030 10 384 4146 or by email at **stps@compulink.gr**

Those interested in volunteering can contact
stps@archelon.gr or visit **www.compulink.gr/stps**
for further information about the society's activities.

useful WEBSITES

You will find internet cafes in the most unlikely of locations on the Ionian Islands. For a relatively modest fee you can surf for an hour - gleaning useful information about onward locations to visit and, sometimes, being able to book transportation or accommodation.

Listed here are some of the more helpful sites that you may wish to visit.

www.athensnews.gr The Athens News used to be produced as a daily English language newspaper and was routinely available not only in Athens but all over Greece. Now it is only published weekly but has been a traditionally useful source of information on such things as impending strikes (ferries, planes, petrol stations and so on). This is its online web version.

www.culture.gr An extensive site from the Greek Ministry of Culture that gives fabulous detail on all the sort of things this guide doesn't cover - museums, archaeological sites, forthcoming cultural events.

www.eatgreektonight.com Want to know how to cook that favourite Greek dish? Need advice on which dishes are suitable for vegetarians? This web site provides recipes for lots of Greek dishes and generates discussion between visitors. Also has some pretty (though somewhat anonymous) photographs to give you the flavour of what a visit to Greece may bestow upon you.

www.ellada.com A massive compendium of useful information about Greece, Greek culture, tourist information and life in general. The extremely lengthy and jumbled index down the left-hand side of the home page is a bit off-putting and the layout could certainly be a bit more imaginative. Still well worth a visit.

www.foi.org.uk This is the website of «Friends of the Ionian», a membership based organisation which supplies some information free of charge but offers a lot more for a (nominal) membership fee. There are also links and message boards. So, even if you're already on holiday on a particular island, it's possible to join and download information of local relevance at a small charge.

www.gnto.gr

www.hri.org/infoxenios/english/ionian Web sites of the Greek National Tourist Organisation. The first is a general site dealing with tourism. Not particularly easy to navigate and aimed more at professional travel trade surfers. The second site is aimed at tourists and provides lots of useful local information. However, it has to be said that this site inevitably presents every place it mentions in glowing terms. Such lavish praise is often undeserved and the site is more useful for its factual information than its opinions.

www.greekislands.gr Complements the GTP site (see below) with lots of useful links and information, principally relating to international ferry services. Also has a list of domestic services but not as useful as GTP. The biggest drawback is the "cheesy" music. Provides a range of other tourism information on railways, camping and so on.

www.greekislandhopping.com Every year, Thomas Cook publishes a useful guide to Greek Island hopping in paperback form, including likely ferry movements for the forthcoming season. This website provides updated information relating to the paperback guide and a host of other useful information. Whilst it's sensible to check that the information is still current before you rely on it for your onward travel, it's a very helpful source of information on the somewhat bewildering and often unreliable world of Greek domestic ferry services.

www.gtpnet.com This is probably the most comprehensive source of information on Greek domestic ferry services - and it tends to be pretty reliable. Easy search facility but, the one down-side, you have to get the

11

spelling exactly the way they've got it. If you're finding this hard to achieve but manage to find either the point of departure or arrival, simply browse and it will throw up all routes for that location.

www.greekwine.gr It isn't all retsina and rocket fuel, honest! This site gives lots of useful information about wineries, growing regions, grapes as well as where you might buy the finished product. The icons look more like signs from the nuclear industry than viniculture but the content is sound and there really are some excellent Greek wines around.

www.islandsofdreams.com An emerging, interactive web portal on Greek Islands, tourism facilities and services. The Ionian is already well covered and more islands and information links are constantly being added.

www.islandstrolling.com A Norwegian site that's also offered in English. The dedicated webmaster here has pulled together lots and lots of useful information and links about Greece and virtually all the Greek Islands. Once you're in the site, scroll down the left hand index until you eventually come to «1000 Links to Greece» click on that to take you to an alphabetic listing of most of the Greek Islands, normally with a selection of several link sites that it's possible for you to visit.

www.ktel.org This is the website of the national bus operator KTEL. Once the site opens, you will find an interactive map. Click on Ionian to see details (unfortunately not comprehensive) of bus services on the various Ionian Islands.

www.olympic-airways.gr

www.aegeanair.com Details of the domestic air services offered by Greece's two main carriers. The hub location is normally Athens. Olympic has more routes whilst Aegean has classier planes. Both operators provide relatively low cost fares. Olympic tends to be cheaper.

www.wunderground.com/global/GR.html Information on worldwide weather. Click on Greece for a three-day forecast by broad geographical area within an interactive weather map.

European blue flag beaches

The European Union implements a scheme to recognise excellence in beach organisation. Known as the Blue Flag, beaches all over Europe apply to receive this award annually and their eligibility is assessed against some twenty-seven separate criteria in the areas of water quality, environmental education and information, environmental management and safety and services. Normally, once a beach has reached the required standard, it tends to continue to receive the award in subsequent years - but each beach has to be re-examined to ensure compliance and sometimes the Blue Flag is rescinded.

Greece currently has 340 Blue Flag Beaches and 5 marinas and the number tends to grow annually. The 27 criteria against which each beach is examined are stringent. For instance, water quality is assessed and requirements forbid the discharge of industrial or sewage related effluent. The local council and beach operator have to organise environmental education activities. There have to be enough litter bins, daily beach cleaning and refuse disposal. First aid has to be available locally along with life saving equipment and personnel. Disabled access and facilities should also be present.

Such a considerable number of detailed environmental considerations should really guarantee that a Blue Flag beach always scores at least at 5* level and probably 5* gold.

However, in the preparation of this edition beach inspections identified that on a number of occasions Blue Flag Beaches in Greece patently did not meet some of the 27 criteria laid down. Yet they had been awarded a Blue Flag. This is a matter of some concern.

Infringements included lack of first aid or lifeguard equipment, lack of disabled access and facilities, sewage discharge into the sea, inadequate signs identifying where to get help in an emergency, inadequate shower or toilet facilities, lifeguards missing during the normal operational hours of 10 a.m. to 6 p.m. and a number of other failures. Had this been the case on just one or two of the beaches inspected, it would perhaps have been understandable but infringements became almost commonplace. Conversely, some Blue Flag beaches provided fully compliant facilities of exceptional quality.

Those who wish to read the full criteria for themselves can view an explanation of all 27 on **www.blueflag.org/Eucriteria** and if you have a concern about the standards on a particular beach you can report it to **hspn@hol.gr** This is the Hellenic Society for the Protection of Nature, the organisation licensed by the EU within Greece to undertake its Blue Flag assessments.

beach**grading**system

How each beach is graded: Each and every beach contained within this book has been inspected at least once and often several times. Beaches are assessed on a scale that awards up to 250 points and allocates one of seven possible grades.

Ten points per item (possible total 100) are added if the beach has:

A Beach Bar or Snack Bar	• Showers
A Clean and Tidy Appearance	• Sunbeds
A Taverna or Restaurant	• Sun Umbrellas
Disabled Access	• Toilets
Litter Bins	• Watersports

Ten points per item (possible total 100) are subtracted if the beach suffers from:

An Unattractive Environment	• Oil or Tar
Glass or Metal on the Sand	• Overcrowding
Litter	• Sewage or Storm Drain Outfalls
No Disabled Access	• Unpleasant Smells
No Facilities	• Weed

An additional award of up to 25 points is made to recognise the ambience of each beach.

An additional award of 25 points is made in recognition of each beach that has secured European Union Blue Flag status.

The seven grades applied can be summarised as follows:

★ :one star **[1 - 50 Points]**

Probably a swamp or a sewage farm. It is virtually impossible to score so low and a beach would have to be in a totally awful state to do so.

★ ★ :two star **[51 - 100 Points]**

Detrimental features, lack of facilities and ambience. Unless you haven't seen your optician recently, you are unlikely to choose to visit this beach.

★ ★ ★ :three star **[101 - 150 Points]**

A reasonable beach to while away a few hours but you mightn't want to stop all day. Will have some facilities but quite possibly some detrimental aspects. Unlikely to possess much ambience or a Blue Flag. The exception will be more isolated beaches with little or no beach organisation. These will score high on ambience but low on facilities.

★ ★ ★ ★ :four star **[151 - 175 Points]**

A well organised beach with few detrimental aspects. Could be an attractive but somewhat isolated beach without lots of facilities. When you get to this level it starts to be about choices - Do you really want to be able to hire a jet ski or go paragliding or would you prefer isolation and solitude?

★ ★ ★ ★ GOLD :four star GOLD **[176 - 200 Points]**

Now you're talking! This is likely to be an excellent beach with a wide range of facilities. You often find very good beaches that haven't yet achieved Blue Flag status in this category. Pleasant but isolated beaches that don't have the level of tourist infrastructure to score additional points also regularly feature.

★ ★ ★ ★ ★ :five star **[201 - 225 Points]**

All Blue Flag beaches should be scoring at this level (but quite a lot don't - so take that as a hint!). Again likely to be a well organised beach with lots of facilities and few, if any, detrimental features. This is likely to be somewhere you'll happily spread your towel for the day.

★ ★ ★ ★ ★ GOLD :five star GOLD **[226 - 250 Points]**

The creme de la creme of beaches. Lots of facilities, invariably a Blue Flag and normally heaps of ambience. If you can't thoroughly enjoy yourself on one of these beaches you need a different type of holiday!

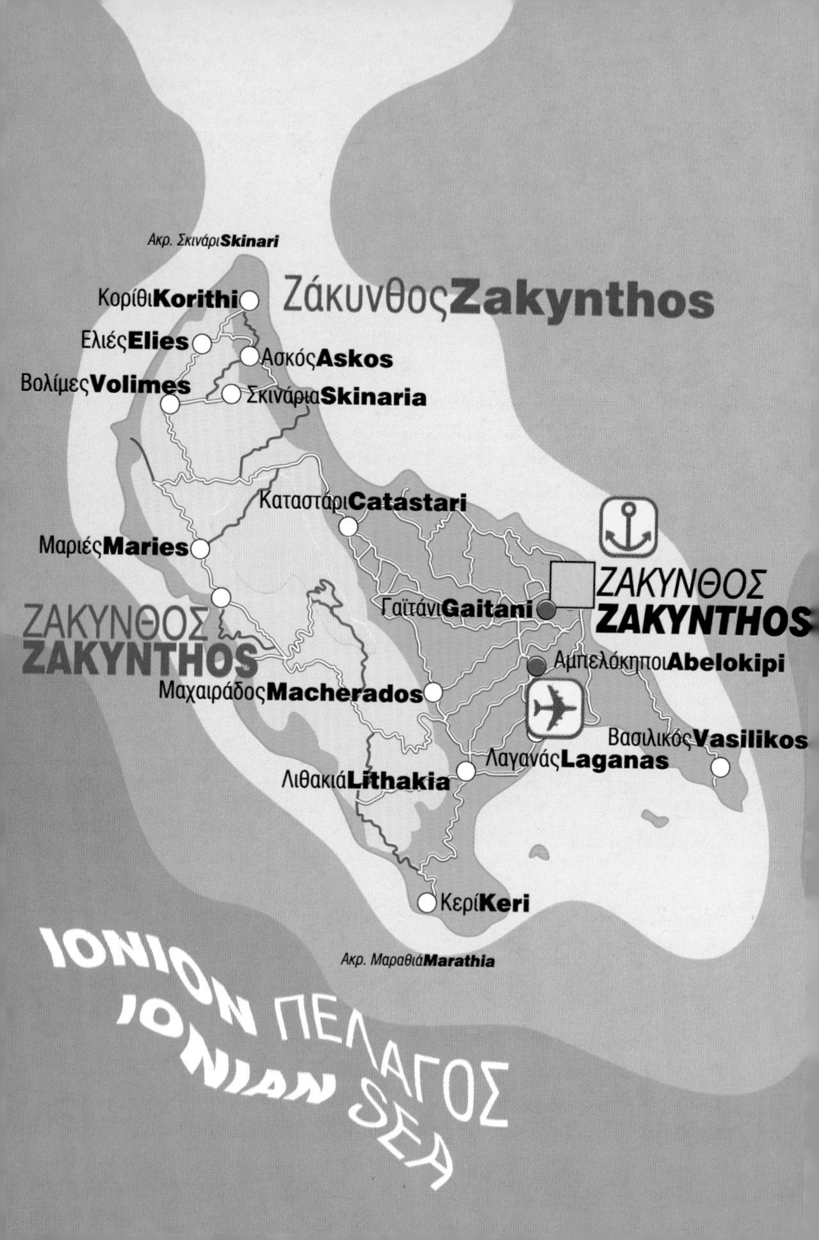

Ακρ. Σκινάρι**Skinari**

Ζάκυνθος**Zakynthos**

Κορίθι**Korithi**

Ελιές**Elies**

Βολίμες**Volimes**

Ασκός**Askos**

Σκινάρια**Skinaria**

Κατάστάρι**Catastari**

Μαριές**Maries**

ΖΑΚΥΝΘΟΣ
ZAKYNTHOS

Γαΐτάνι**Gaitani**

ΖΑΚΥΝΘΟΣ
ZAKYNTHOS

Αμπελάκηποι**Abelokipi**

Μαχαιράδος**Macherados**

Βασιλικός**Vasilikos**

Λιθακιά**Lithakia**

Λαγανάς**Laganas**

Κερί**Keri**

Ακρ. Μαραθιά**Marathia**

IONION ΠΕΛΑΓΟΣ
IONIAN SEA

about
zakynthos

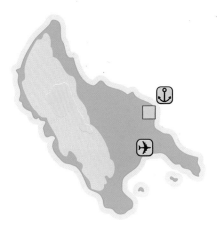

☐ introduction

☐ **general**information

☐ **practical**information

☐ zakynthos**resorts**

☐ zakynthos**beaches**

In less than twenty years, Zakynthos has developed from a sleepy agricultural backwater -virtually reliant on the grape and the olive - into the second most popular tourist destination in the Ionian, and the fourth most popular in Greece. Its tiny population of 40,000 is totally outnumbered by the annual incursion of well over 500,000 tourists.

Yet, there is no island in Greece which takes its responsibility for your enjoyment more seriously. The Greeks admirably describe their philosophy in a word - "Xenos" - meaning both stranger and guest. And that's the average tourist's experience of Zakynthos; an island of hospitality, sunshine and smiles where you are welcomed like a member of the family - a guest rather than a stranger.

Zakynthos is doubly blessed with a wonderfully warm summer climate and enough winter rain to guarantee its fertility throughout the rest of the year. This is no scraggy, barren, rock-crop but an island so rich in greenery you would be forgiven for thinking you were in the forests of Wales or France. Only scrutiny of the main crops - olives, grapes, lemons, tomatoes and the hot summer sun overhead gives the lie to this illusion.

The sense of smell runs riot here. Whether the cause is the cascading trellis of bougainvillea or honeysuckle outside your hotel; the carpet of herbs and wild flowers surrounding your apartment; the citrus tang of ripening lemons wafting on a warm breeze or simply the burnt wood aroma of your dinner as it spit roasts over the charcoal at the local taverna.

It should not be forgotten that this island, having endured the ravages of occupation in the Second World War, was to be devastated by a dreadful earthquake in 1953.Thus there are few antiquities to see. Most of the buildings have been sympathetically reconstructed, and work is even in hand to reconstruct the Casino - previously the centre-piece of the town's bustling Saint Mark's Square.

There are relatively few resorts on Zakynthos, although some of the newer ones are rapidly expanding. Laganas, once little more than a golden beach, is now massive and a home for those who seek fun and late-night entertainment. Tiny Keri conversely beckons to those who enjoy peace, scenery and exploration. For those prepared to investigate beyond the hotel swimming pool, there are treasures to discover all over Zakynthos. Whether it's a secret beach, hill climbing, old churches, Venetian ruins or local crafts; Zakynthos will surely oblige.

aWHISTLE-STOP history of Zakynthos

This is a proud island and its people are fiercely protective. Nevertheless, history demonstrates that it has been subject to almost continual occupation and its inhabitants to dreadful oppression, from the earliest days right into the 20th century. Some would argue that the latest occupiers are the tourists themselves!

Its pre - Christian history seems to commence with the legend that it was occupied by Ulysses (he of the Homeric narrative - king of neighbouring Ithaca). Ulysses is more renowned for his participation in the Trojan War but apparently conquered the island somewhere along the way, compelling its inhabitants to assist him in his predatory campaigns.

From approximately 500 BC the island enjoyed a relatively peaceful existence for a couple of centuries until the world conquering Romans occupied it, the rest of Greece and indeed extended their grasping tentacles to most of the then civilised world.

The fall of the Roman Empire was not to bring stability for the inhabitants of Zakynthos. Byzantine conquerors arrived only to be ousted by Vandals. Saracens followed, subsequently attracting the attention of Crusaders who must have lost their bearings for the Holy Land, liked what they saw and decided to stay. Local fable also has it that Mary Magdalene had experienced similar difficulties while on an evangelical mission, several centuries earlier.

A Norman conquest was followed by round two of the Byzantine Butchery Brigade. Even the sacking of Constantinople did not prevent occupation by a series of other marauderers. By the twelfth century fertile Zakynthos was being mercilessly raped. Its population was subjected to the most dreadful abuse and life became intolerable. This period of overt slavery continued for some centuries until the mid 15th century.

Improved communication made the powerful and somewhat distant neighbours, the Venetians, aware of the island's plight. And you only have to look at a map to realise why they might take an interest in the situation. Recognising the strategic importance of the Ionian Sea for their own self preservation, they had soon evicted an occupying Turkish force and mounted a protective occupation of the island themselves. The hillside fortress (did anyone tell you there is still a Kastro high on the hill above the town?) is a tangible reminder of this, the Zakynthian renaissance.

The Venetians were the first occupier to give rather than take. It was the Venetians who imported and, so successfully, cultivated the olive. Many of the existing trees are centuries old. The humble vine was similarly planted in the fertile Zakynthian soil. The hillside fortress gradually became a township and eventually the town was to spread into the area of the present day port, as Venetian soldiers and other refugees from the Turkish invasion of the Southern Aegean were encouraged to settle on the island.

Zakynthos was later to receive the attention of French revolutionaries who appeared on the island in 1797. Temporarily evicted by Russian and Turkish fleets, they were to return in 1807. Bonaparte's troops occupied the island, but who was at war with Bonaparte? Yes, you've guessed it, Zakynthos became a British acquisition in 1810 and this lasted till 1864.The British occupation was ruthless, mercenary and cruelly maintained. The English may have brought cricket to the Ionian but they also brought with them the gallows.

Many of the island's young, wealthy, intelligentsia escaped the cruel regime by travelling. It's amazing what the British condoned in the name of education and enlightenment and these "Grand Tours" were actually encouraged. In 1821 a group of young intelligentsia was to return to the island, banding themselves into an organisation known as the "Filiki Etairia". Their vow - to rid the Ionian of all foreign oppressors - was to take many years to accomplish. When the English foolishly sided with predatory Turks against the local community, it was like lighting the blue touch paper but not standing clear! British expulsion became inevitable.

However, there were to be more major historical hiccups destined to thwart the peaceful habitation of this serene island. The Nazi ravages of the early 1940's were not to leave the island unscarred. German and Italian occupation took place between 1941 and 1944, leaving a temporary blot on the island's peaceful horizon. Civil war was to follow, lasting until the late 1940's.

Perhaps the most momentous sadness of all was caused not by mankind but by nature. 1953 witnessed the most dreadful day in Zakynthian history. August the 12th was to mark the day on which virtually the whole island was to be felled by a catastrophic earthquake. Virtually every building was affected - most beyond repair. Many of the population were killed or injured. Fires spread across the island and laid waste the port.

Only time will reveal whether Zakynthos has faced its last hostility or whether, in reality, the advent of significant tourism is the latest predator to confront it. It is to be hoped that the islanders will, on this occasion, be able to control the incursion. What a tragedy if free-falling economic expansion becomes the final destructive influence to wreak havoc on this fertile and friendly paradise.

cultural**HERITAGE**

For an island that lost so much of its history to the earthquake's grasp, it was perhaps inevitable that the islanders would jealously hoard all remaining artefacts. While there are no significant sites and few buildings of note, Zakynthos is relatively well endowed with museums and centres of culture, as the following listings reveal.

Civic Art Gallery: Located at the back of magnificent Solomos Square, this majestic gallery features upwards of 1,000 beautiful icons - many from the Byzantine rather than the Microsoft period! There are also sculptures and religious carvings. It is open six days per week and tends to close early. Admission charge.

Cultural Heritage Centre: Also in Solomos Square, close to the harbour walls, this is home to the civic library - consisting of many thousands of volumes - together with pictorial and photographic evidence of the island's previous life. Many of the photographs predating the earthquake are particularly fascinating. There is also a theatre cum ballroom which is used for ad - hoc displays and entertainments. The area outside the centre is used for visiting exhibitions. At other times, it hosts a cafeteria. Unfortunately, over the last few years Zakynthos has lost both of its two remaining outdoor cinemas. With the exception of videos or Sky TV at your hotel or local bar, the Cultural Centre is probably the only place on the island where you may be able to see a half decent film.

Solomos Museum: The Solomos Museum is a relatively inconspicuous building next to the bank in St. Mark's Square. It is dedicated to the Greek national poet, Dionysos Solomos, author of the epic poem "Hymn to Liberty" (the Greek national anthem) and arguably Zakynthos' most famous son. His remains are contained in a mausoleum within the museum, which also features displays relating to other famous Zakynthians (including British ex-patriates). Open most days. Free admission. Closes early.

Venetian Fortress "KASTRO": Dispel any ideas you may have of an English castle. This walled site of Venetian occupation is now home to a thickly pined forest which covers the whole of the hillside above the town. There are remains of several buildings such as a cathedral, jail and ammunition store. Beware; the site is peppered with deep well shafts dug in readiness for long sieges.

A stiff 3km uphill walk from the town and through the leafy residential area of Bohali brings you to the fortress. Alternately, a taxi will have you there in five minutes and the castle is on the itinerary of some island excursions. To do it justice, come under your own steam and stay as long as you need to explore it fully.

This is a great retreat from the beach when it's too hot and a super excursion for the kids. Watch out for the wells and wear sensible shoes. A parental hand is advised when walking the walls; it's a long drop!

Open six days per week but only until the mid afternoon. Admission charge.

Volimes Craft Village: The craft village of Volimes is well worth a trip, even though your bottom will be extremely saddle sore if travelling on two wheeled transport! Located about 30 km. north of Zakynthos Town, you will know you've arrived as countless local inhabitants throw themselves in front of your car in order to persuade you to stop and purchase!

Offerings vary from local honey, nuts and olive oil through to tapestries, rugs, lace table cloths, pottery, clocks and an assortment of other trinkets and treasures.

Aghios Dionysos: Focal point of the western end of the harbour, the extremely large Saint Dennis' church is highly visible, even as your ferry enters the harbour. This beautiful building, with its separate rectangular bell tower, contains many fine relics and icons relating to the island's patron saint, Dionysos. It stands in its own square, close to the water's edge. Outside, street hawkers ply their wares, varying from religious icons to hot corn on the cob. Tourists present on the 24th August will witness the special celebrations held in honour of the saint.

St. Nicholas of the Mole: Located beyond the Heritage Centre in Solomos Square, this is a very photogenic church. The bell tower dates from the 17th century and the church itself is associated with Saint Dionysos who preached on the site in the 16th century, prior to becoming Abbot of Anafonitria Monastery.

Catholic Church of St. Mark: The small, inconspicuous church of Saint Mark occupies a quiet corner of the square to which it gives its name. "Platia Aghios Markos" is the focal point of island life and has become the main town square - populated by bustling cafe bars and restaurants. Located next to the Solomos Museum, it is not a particular find but provides a cool retreat on hot summer days when curiosity, or heatstroke, overtakes you.

Church of St. Maura at Macherado: Finding Saint Maura will take you some 15 kilometres into the western interior of the island. Journeys are possible by bus but, as these are designed more with the travelling needs of the local population than tourists in mind, you will probably prefer your own transport or a taxi. The belfry is of interest but it is principally the miraculous properties of the Icon of Saint Maura which commands attention. Other relics within the church are reputed to date from the 13th century.

Those making their own way can follow a number of routes but the most direct is probably the western arterial road which leads to Kiliomeno. Here, the central church is also worth a visit and you can climb the bell tower if you're really daring.

There is also a monastery at Macherado where visitors are welcomed between 9.00 a.m. and 3.30 p.m. and 6.00 p.m. until 9.00 p.m.

Anafonitria Monastery: Located in the north-west of the island, enormous unofficial signposts will ultimately point you towards Anafonitria and the Smugglers' Wreck. Turn towards the village or you will find yourself travelling a significant number of kilometres extra and arriving at the craft village of Volimes instead.

The village road gives out at the very monastery door. Do not believe the huge signs pointing you towards the Smugglers' Wreck. They are a fancy in the eye of the sign writer and the only way they will take you to the Wreck or to nearby Porto Vromi is if you possess a trial bike, extra strong nerves and a hell of a lot of luck. If you want to see the wreck, do yourself a favour and take the boat trip.

The monastery (and indeed the picturesque village) is well worthy of your time. Reputedly dating from the 15th century, and certainly looking that old, it has some spectacular murals. Here Saint Dionysos spent a reclusive 38 years as abbot. A number of items associated with his lengthy sojourn are retained in the monastery. Or, to use the words of a colourful local guidebook "He was born in 1547 and at an early age he became a mink in the monastery of Anafonitria". Furs, fur, Saint Dennis!

culture

ISLANDtravel

There are plenty of ways to travel to and around Zakynthos. It's also possible to journey onwards to other parts of Greece, via Patras or Athens, and to island hop throughout the Ionian via Cephalonia. Although the Ionian is notorious for its lack of island hopping facilities, on Zakynthos you do have a few options.

Air travel: Scheduled air travel is currently available only via Olympic Airways to Athens and once or twice per week to Cephalonia. The Cephalonia route has the distinction of being the shortest scheduled route in Europe - seven minutes airborne. The route used to be completely separate but now tends to be a twice per week diversion, associated with the Athens itinerary. It's projected that private airlines may soon organise Ionian domestic routes but at the moment it's Olympic or swim!

Arrival at Athens is now into the new Eleftherios Venizelos Airport (Spata) and no longer involves a transfer between airports for your onward flight. The new airport is 500% better than the old one at Helinikon albeit, it has to be said, that it lacks the old airport's character. The journey from the airport into central Athens costs about three euro on the express coach and you can continue to use the ticket around Athens for 24 hours. As it's nearly 30 kilometres from Athens, travel by taxi is more expensive than it used to be and some of the drivers will try to rip you off! Get a price first. As they battle to complete a motorway and rail link to the airport, traffic is almost permanently snarled up - so allow plenty of time for your journey. There's also an express coach for Piraeus and another for Rafina, should you be travelling on to other Aegean islands by boat.

Most flights are currently undertaken with ATP 70 seat planes in a journey time of about one hour. Those flights which touch down on Cephalonia, however, add at least another 30 minutes to the overall flight time between Zakynthos and Athens. Prices are reasonable, with the cost of a return ticket between Athens and Zakynthos costing under £100. Check in time is one hour ahead of departure but you will routinely be boarded with only minutes to spare. Punctuality is not a strong point of this service!

Travel from the UK and other major European destinations direct to Zakynthos is only available by charter flight in the season, which routinely means early May to late October. Prices vary according to month but there are often bargains to be had. Indirect flights via Athens are available all year round. The cheapest UK route to Athens is probably Easy Jet although other carriers are now becoming far more competitive than previously.

Buses: The national bus company, KTEL, operates a fleet of single deck buses from its bus station located at Filita, just behind the main supermarket and the police station on the waterfront promenade. Recognisable by their dingy blue and cream livery, these "coaches" are more suited to the early morning farm run up the island's interior than fast transportation to Athens.

You may well find that the bus that took you to the beach is gearing up for the seven hour slog to Athens, but at least it's cheap and you will certainly experience the colour of travel Greek style! You'll also discover what it's like to be a casserole in a slow cooker and what happens to the blood supply to your nether regions after four hours on a hard seat. Still, thousands love it every week, so why shouldn't you? Alternately, there are inclusive excursions, invariably including an overnight stop in Athens, which can work out good value (although the quality of accommodation is sometimes less than sparkling). Make sure your accommodation is at least C class and preferably B or A.

Travel round the island by bus is fun, although it's more intended for the local population and the timetable reflects this with a preponderance of early morning and late afternoon timings. The main resorts - Alikes, Argassi, Kalamaki, Laganas and Tsilivi are served reasonably well and it is possible to journey, for instance, right down the Vasilikos peninsula to Porto Roma or to the northernmost tip of the island, Volimes by more occasional routes. Beyond this, travel is limited in the main to the inland villages.

While the resort timetable is routinely displayed at the main bus station in English, the less touristy routes tend only to be written up in Greek. Enquire inside for details. Bus stops are now more plentiful around the island - watch out for white pictures of a single deck bus on a blue background with the word "Stassis".

The interior buses, in particular, are not recommended for those of a nervous disposition. Destinations such as Lithakia, Kiliomeno and Romiri undoubtedly sound very romantic - and they are. However, the combination of 100 decibel Greek profanities, hair pin bends, much horn pounding, three out of four sets of wheels still on the road (most of the time) and the odd herd of goats in the way can simply be too much for those of a nervous disposition.

Ferries: Zakynthos relies on daily ferries for its very life blood. There are two routes. The main one links with mainland Killini on the Peloponnese; features several departures daily and takes just over an hour. The second is a much smaller ferry, utilising one boat twice daily between Northern Zakynthos and Pessada in southern Cephalonia. The boat departs from a small harbour at St. Nicholas Bay (Skinari), just beyond Volimes. From here, the whole of the Ionian is your oyster with onward routes to Ithaca, Lefkas, Meganissi, Paxos and Corfu. The only slight complication is that you have to travel by road from Pessada to one of several other harbours located on Cephalonia to catch your onward ferry.

Boats are seldom full, except in the high season. August tends to be a nightmare and you must book in advance at this time. Services are suspended in bad weather except in fog, when the journey is completed much faster than the normal scheduled journey time!

Hire cars and Motor Bikes: There are a large number of auto-rental agencies on Zakynthos. Of late, the standard has improved significantly. Greek insurance - even when collision damage waiver has been purchased - is not automatically comprehensive and motor bikes are seldom rented with full insurance. Tyres and wheels are frequently uninsurable and this is worth bearing in mind before you undertake any dare devil dirt track riding.

Accidents can mean big bills, potential court appearances and even the confiscation of your passport until your fine is paid. Make sure you are fully insured. Tourist offences tend to be tolerated by the police but a stricter attitude is being taken with the significant growth of vehicles on the island. Five years ago there were no traffic lights on Zakynthos. Now there are several sets. Oddly, the now perpetual jams along the harbour road only arrived following the installation of the lights!

The main international rental agencies are well represented on Zakynthos and there are also some local agencies. These tend to be cheaper without any major reduction in rental conditions. Minimum rental ages for drivers are usually 21 or 25, depending on the category of vehicle hired. A valid licence must normally have been held for at least twelve months. Hire charges are quite high compared with other European destinations and you may even find it cheaper to make arrangements in the UK, via your travel agent. This is particularly the case in high season. Once in the resort, you will find that prices are negotiable and probably best booked direct with an agency where you can examine the small print. Discounts for longer hire periods are routinely offered and should always be negotiated for more than one day's hire. You can even book on the internet.

Motor bikes will often be offered at a far younger age and without production of a valid licence. A tour around the casualty queue at the local hospital will reveal the folly of hiring motor bikes without previous experience (and valid insurance). The roads on Zakynthos are not for the untutored. Frequent pot holes and protruding rocks, unsurfaced tracks and the effect of winds on certain roads comprise major hazards. Add to this the laid back attitude towards drink driving and the almost universal failure to wear crash helmets and you will begin to understand why renting motor bikes, in particular, should only be attempted by experienced riders.

Those hiring bikes should consider their needs carefully. A small moped is fine for transport between your apartment and the beach or that more distant taverna. However, it will not be suitable for trips through the hilly north of the island and journeys down the Vasilikos Peninsula. A larger bike or motor scooter with gears will take you up most hill roads. Rates tend to be comparable between agencies but you can haggle, especially for longer hire periods.

Motor Boats and Sailing Dinghies: Motor boats and sailing dinghies can be hired at the main and some smaller resorts. Boats are a potential way of visiting nearby beaches and also the small islets such as Marathonisi and Pelouzon. However, it is most advisable to be conversant with the craft you hire as the offshore currents are tricky, even for the

29

locals. Some folks use jet skis to visit the islets but this is an extremely expensive indulgence.

Few regulations seem to govern the hire of such equipment. You will probably not be asked to justify your expertise in controlling the particular craft under hire. You should be supplied with a life preserver for each passenger - a legal requirement in Greece - and you should ensure that you know the insurance implications if things go wrong. It's not simply what you might owe for damage to the boat but also a case of what insurance do you have if, for instance, you injure one of your passengers, a swimmer or a turtle? Check anticipated weather conditions and always let someone know where you're going and your anticipated time of return.

For those who favour sea travel without the hazard of hiring your own boat, a very cost effective option is to take one of the many round the island trips which leave daily. More localised trips around the Blue Caves and Keri Caves are offered from relevant harbours. These trips are heavily marketed by tour reps and from kiosks in the main resorts and the promenade in the town (Strada Marina). Again, checking your carrier is properly insured, carries sufficient life preservers and is not overloaded, makes great sense.

The round the island tours take up to ten hours to complete and offer good value. However, families need to assess whether younger children will become bored with only occasional stops for swimming. Cover from the incessant sun is a necessity as is plenty of sun lotion for liberal application throughout the day. Taking babies on such trips is not advisable There is no doubt that this is one of the most relaxing ways to see the island's coastline and to visit one or two of the more inaccessible spots, such as Smugglers' Wreck and Porto Vromi.

Pedal Cycles: Pedal cycles, tandems and four seater bikes can be hired in most of the larger resorts and the main town. Again, check for insurance obligations. You are probably liable for loss, theft or damage. Most bikes tend to be solid but ungeared. This is O.K. for downhill but not so wonderful for rising gradients! Pedal bikes are a great way to get around the flatter resorts but the hilly nature of the island needs to be borne in mind by those considering more extensive excursions.

Many cycles will be hired with luggage panniers and child seats although you may have to ask. Make sure you get a puncture kit, suitable spanners and a chain lock. Bike hire tends to be localised and, therefore, note the depot phone number carefully before embarking on distant journeys, just in case ………

Cycling to the northern parts of the island is not recommended. The hills and distances are just too much. Those staying in Argassi or Kalamaki might fancy a bike ride down the Vasilikos peninsula. It's possible but you will be exhausted with the roller-coaster hill roads.

Taxis: Considering how expensive it is to rent a car, taxi hire comes as a pleasant surprise. A full taxi (and there is no such thing as a full taxi on Zakynthos!) can work out much cheaper than car hire and even beat the bus for shorter journeys.

Prices are cheaper than the UK and many other European countries. However, you need to get a few of the rules straight before setting out. Firstly, you pay from the point the taxi departs from. So, if you book one at your hotel and it has to travel there to collect you, expect to pay more than hiring one in the road outside. Certain journeys are (quite unfathomably) charged at an excess rate. Going to the airport is charged at a fixed rate, for instance. Journeys after midnight may well see the imposition of a doubled fare.

One feature which people just freak out over is shared taxi syndrome. The driver will stop and collect additional fares until the cab is full. The additional passengers will pay the routine fare for their portion of the journey. However, you will also pay for the same ground covered and for the additional bits when you travelled on your own. Considering the low prices paid, this seems a fair compromise in all the circumstances.

Also noteworthy is the shrine like interior of each cab. These icons would grace most churches on the island with their worry beads, Madonna figurines, crucifixes, etc., etc., Only the Vatican can surely boast a better collection. Still, if it makes you feel safer travelling…….

As there are in excess of 100 cabs operating on the island, supply is usually plentiful. There are less around between midnight and the early morning, during afternoon siesta and rain showers. There are none at all when there's football of any significance on the television!

zakynthos

resorts

ZAKYNTHOSresorts

Alykanas *Αλικανάς*

Resort location/description: A growing resort that is now entwined with big sister Alykes. A little quieter, with most accommodation located away from the beach. (Some is on the main road, attracting noise). Located about 20km. north of Zakynthos Town on the north east coast, Alykanas and Alykes are the last two major tourist outposts before you encounter the more rugged and sparsely populated mountain areas. Pick your accommodation with care and you will be rewarded with a relaxing environment whilst plenty of facilities are located close by.

Taxis/public transport: Buses and taxis serve the resort.

Banks and cash machines: No. Neighbouring Alykes possesses an ATM cluster.

Currency exchange: Exchange money at supermarkets, hotels and tourist offices.

Hotels and accommodation: Mainly smaller hotels with a range of self-catering accommodation available. Much is pre-let to tour companies but you should be able to get accommodation without difficulty throughout the season.

Shops: Mainly tourist offerings. The laundry is very useful!

Supermarkets: Several mini-markets.

Chemist/pharmacy: No. Nearest is at Katastari Village about 4 km. away.

Disabled friendly: The resort is flat and some beaches are accessible. Other beaches are approached down steps and unsuitable for wheelchairs.

Doctors/medical centre: No.

Petrol station: On the main road between Alykes and Alykanas.

Car hire: Yes.

Bike hire: Motor bikes and pedal cycles.

Police station: No. Nearest is at Katastari.

Restaurants: A reasonable variety for a small resort - including Indian and Chinese.

Tavernas: Mainly tourist offerings in the resort but there are a few gems in the surrounding villages. Explore!

Nightclubs/discos: No.
Atmosphere: Relatively quiet. More suited to those who enjoy walking. Possesses a family atmosphere.
Drinking water: Drink bottled except in hotels.
Interruptions to electricity supply: Sometimes.
Torch needed: Advisable if you intend to walk beyond the village boundary.
Cinema: No. Local bars show films or Sky TV.
Golf course: No.
Resort environment: Lack of immediate access to a beach may be seen as a problem by some. Otherwise pleasant, family orientated resort, nestling in the attractive countryside and surrounded by interesting places to explore and good walking opportunities.
Nearest beach: Three or four to choose from within 1km. of the main resort.
Ferries: Zakynthos Town for mainland Killini. Skinari (Ag. Nikolaos) for Cephalonia.
Distance from airport: 25 km.
Boat mooring: A small and very limited harbour is situated at Ag. Kiriaki, about 1 km. from the resort.
Any other comments: This is a pleasant resort if a beach is not your greatest priority. Don't come here for bags of night-life and a dozen different high volume nightclubs. Use this as a base for exploration to see the old Zakynthos, discover the countryside and taste some real taverna food.

Alykes
ΑΛΙΚΕΣ

Resort location/description: This is the furthest north that residential tourism extends on Zakynthos. A relatively large resort, located on the north-east coast and some twenty-five kilometres beyond Zakynthos Town. In addition to its attractive beach and pleasant river (yes, a river!), Alykes possesses a good range of tourist facilities and places to eat. It's an ideal location from which to tour the mountainous northern part of Zakynthos and even to reach Cephalonia. Its one down side is the existence of somewhat smelly salt-pans just behind the resort and a little too close to some of the accommodation for comfort!
Taxis/public transport: Buses and taxis.
Banks and cash machines: There is now an ATM cash machine cluster on the main road through the resort.

Currency exchange: Hotels, supermarkets and tourist offices will all oblige.

Hotels and accommodation: Mainly small to medium sized hotels with some self catering accommodation extending back into the surrounding countryside.

Shops: A selection of tourist offerings. For more locally orientated supplies visit neighbouring Katastari Village.

Supermarkets: Mainly small mini-markets placed strategically at a few locations within the resort.

Chemist/pharmacy: No. Nearest is at Katastari 2 km. distant.

Disabled friendly: This is a flat resort with wheelchair access routinely available to the beach. Gradients begin to rise immediately you leave the resort and the northern region of Zakynthos is, of course, quite mountainous.

Doctors/medical centre: No.

Petrol station: On the main road between Alykes and Alykanas. Further station near Katastari.

Car hire: Yes.

Bike hire: Motor bikes and pedal cycles.

Police station: Nearest is at Katastari.

Restaurants: Plenty. Most are Greek or Italian influence. However, there's also Indian and Chinese (on the same menu!).

Tavernas: Tavernas within the resort tend to be tourist orientated. However, there are some gems in the surrounding villages and it's well worth exploring.

Nightclubs/discos: There may be 1 or 2 on the outskirts, there may not! Otherwise, the emphasis is on music bars that offer the opportunity to party at least beyond the witching hour.

Atmosphere: A beach - eat - sleep type of resort. Calming yet well connected with the rest of the island. Good point to base yourself in order to explore. Relatively quiet but with sufficient life to be able to enjoy yourself. Not a place to party till dawn but doesn't bed down at 9 p.m. either.

Drinking water: Drink bottled except in hotels.

Interruptions to electricity supply: Occasional.

Torch needed: Only if you intend to explore beyond the resort boundaries.

Cinema: No. Some bars offer Sky Films and Sport.

Golf course: No.

Resort environment: This is still discernibly Greece. A quiet, pleasant family resort with an excellent beach and attractive surroundings (except the salt pans). Enough night life without going over the top into disco heaven.

Nearest beach: Resort, 0 - 1 km depending on your accommodation.

Ferries: Zakynthos Town for the route to mainland Killini. Ag. Nikolaos (Skinari) for the Cephalonia route.

Distance from airport: 25 km.

Boat mooring: No. There is limited opportunity at the harbour located between Alykes and Alykanas. Very small craft may also be able to moor in the river.

Any other comments: A good place from which to visit the local wineries. Now has its own tourist "train" that motors around the area - saving that foot leather. Excellent location from which to explore. Relatively quiet but certainly not asleep.

Argassi *Αργάσι*

Resort location/description: Argassi is a sprawling coastal strip, now meandering back into pleasant, surrounding foothills. Gateway to the beautiful Vassilikos Peninsula, it's a good resort to explore from - located approximately 4 km. from both the main town and the airport. Follow the Vassilikos road from Zakynthos town - hugging the coastline as tight as you can - to reach the resort in about ten minutes.

Taxis/public transport: There is a reasonably frequent bus service and a constant procession of taxis, prowling the main road and resort.

Banks and cash machines: No. The nearest facilities are at Zakynthos Town.

Currency exchange: Hotels, supermarkets, travel offices and currency exchanges all change money.

Hotels and accommodation: Argassi possesses a range of small to medium size, low rise hotels. There are also basic rooms and more sophisticated self catering accommodation to rent. Much of the accommodation is pre-let to tour companies but you will still routinely find accommodation - except perhaps in August, when it's advisable to pre-book.

Shops: A selection of shops, principally aimed at the needs of the tourist.

Supermarkets: A selection of small mini-markets is peppered through the resort. For a large supermarket, you have to travel to Zakynthos Town.

Chemist/pharmacy: Yes. On the main road as you enter the resort, located on the seaward side of the road.

Disabled friendly: Relatively. The resort is flat in most places and even access to the beach is possible at certain spots. However, some of the accommodation is set in the surrounding foothills, up relatively steep roads. It's advisable to check the location before booking.

Doctors/medical centre: Yes.

Petrol station: Yes, one on the main road in the village and two or three more on the outskirts.

Car hire: Yes.

Bike hire: Motor bikes and pedal cycles.

Police station: No. Nearest is on the corner of the harbour road in the main town.

Restaurants: A wide selection including Chinese, Indian and other exotic offerings that come and go by the season.

Tavernas: Mainly of the tourist variety, although there are a few authentic ones outside of the village (if you know where to look). There's also a fair range of Greek "souvlaki" take-away offerings and other establishments selling sandwiches, burgers and the like.

Nightclubs/discos: One or two on the periphery of the resort that come, and just as quickly go, by the season. Main provision is music bars that stay open until late and may even have a small dance floor.

Atmosphere: Friendly. A place to party and enjoy yourself. Not for those who prefer solitude. The beach is a bit of a let-down and most people take the free buses to one or other of the offerings on the Vassilikos Peninsula. A relatively large resort with facilities to match.

Drinking water: Use bottled except in the hotels.

Interruptions to electricity supply: Not very frequent but they do happen!

Torch needed: No.

Cinema: No. Many bars show current Sky Films and Sport.

Golf course: No.

Resort environment: While you are on the resort's main drag, it's just another tourist enclave and nothing to write home about. However, walk up into the surrounding foothills and all this changes with fabulous views down to the bay and beyond. You can even walk across the foothills to the neighbouring resort of Kalamaki.

Nearest beach: Resort. Although it has to be said this is one of Argassi's failings. The narrowest of strip beaches serves the tourist population poorly and most people prefer to use a hotel or apartment complex pool. It's either that or journey several kilometres to the Vassilikos Peninsula, which has a range of sparkling beaches to entice you.

Ferries: Nearest ferry service is from Zakynthos Town to mainland Killini.

Distance from airport: 4 km.

Boat mooring: No. Nearest harbour is at Zakynthos Town.

Any other comments: Basks in the warm sun for most of the season.

Scented flora surrounds many of the properties as any walk through the resort will amply demonstrate. Home to the "Fun Castle...Wacky Warehouse...Reptile House and Kids' Farm". Come to Argassi to be entertained. Don't come if you prefer your own company. Indeed the resort even has two large bouzoukia. So if you like Greek music and throwing flowers at 30 euro a tray, Argassi's your place!

Kalamaki Καλαμάκι

Resort location/description: Accessed from the main roads that lead here from Zakynthos, Argassi and Laganas, Kalamaki lies an equidistant 5km from each. This is the nearest resort to the airport (so like planes or suffer). A pleasant enough resort although it is now growing rapidly and development, regrettably, could be getting out of control. Restrictions prevent building near the beach as it is a breeding ground for the Loggerhead turtle. So large hotel complexes with one or even two pools are springing up behind the beach instead! Not unpleasant but will need to be watched over the next few years to see whether it chooses the same route as neighbouring Laganas.

Taxis/public transport: Buses and taxis serve the resort.

Banks and cash machines: No. Nearest facilities are Laganas or Zakynthos Town.

Currency exchange: Hotels, shops, tourist offices and a host of others will spring to assist you.

Hotels and accommodation: Small to medium size hotels plus a selection of self catering complexes and more humble rooms.

Shops: Geared to the tourist but in reasonable quantity.

Supermarkets: Mainly small mini markets and spread through the resort.

Chemist/pharmacy: Yes. On the outskirts of the village along the road towards Laganas.

Disabled friendly: The resort is flat and many of the hotels have pools. However, the beach itself is not accessible for wheelchairs.

Doctors/medical centre: No. Nearest provision is Laganas, Argassi or Zakynthos Town.

Petrol station: On the outskirts of the village about 2 km. along the airport road or the Argassi road.

Car hire: Yes.

Bike hire: Pedal cycles and motor bikes

Police station: No. Nearest is on the harbour road in the main town.

Restaurants: A wide variety including Chinese and Indian. There are also some good, upmarket Greek offerings.

Tavernas: One or two authentic ones - particularly on the outskirts of the resort. The rest are mainly of the tourist variety.

Nightclubs/discos: One hillside disco. Lots of music bars - some with dance floors. If the urge to dance at 110 decibels is driving you, pop next door to Laganas.

Atmosphere: This is a resort for lazy days by the sea or in the pool with a fair range of night life to occupy you in the evenings. There are pleasant hillside, and olive grove, walks. Good eating opportunities abound (with a little careful research).

Drinking water: Drink bottled except in hotels.

Interruptions to electricity supply: Occasional.

Torch needed: Only if your accommodation is beyond the village boundary.

Cinema: No. Some bars show current films and Sky TV.

Golf course: No.

Resort environment: This is still a relatively pleasant resort which spreads over a wide area. Currently there's plenty of space between its various facilities but there are signs of "infilling". Hopefully it will not make the mistakes of neighbour Laganas.

Nearest beach: Resort. 0 - 1 km. depending on accommodation.

Ferries: Zakynthos Town hosts the main route to Killini on the Peloponnese.

Distance from airport: 3 km.

Boat mooring: No.

Any other comments: Still discernibly Greek (at least in the main area of the resort). Kalamaki is flower filled, with olive groves carpeted in herbs and pleasant traditional restaurants to discover. It's a good place for country and hillside walks and an attractive beach location. Maybe you'll even spot a Loggerhead turtle.

Keri
Κερί

Resort location/description: Keri is little more than a fishing village that realised, a decade ago, that there was more money to be made transporting tourists round the local caves than by catching fish. Located on the west coast, towards the centre of the island, Keri has good road links with the main town whilst, at the same time, possessing splendid isolation in a picturesque, picture-postcard location.

Taxis/public transport: Occasional buses. Telephone for a taxi.

Banks and cash machines: No.

Currency exchange: A couple of the tourist offices and shops will oblige but it's strictly limited. Main provision is in Zakynthos Town.

Hotels and accommodation: No hotels to speak of. The odd pension and a cluster of self catering accommodation.

Shops: A few shops providing basic necessities and more tourist orientated offerings.

Supermarkets: One or two mini-markets.

Chemist/pharmacy: No.

Disabled friendly: Keri is relatively flat around the area of the beach and harbour. However, there are rising gradients at the outskirts of the resort. It is possible to get a wheelchair onto the pebble beach with a bit of a struggle.

Doctors/medical centre: No.

Petrol station: One in the village and another 2 km. down the main road.

Car hire: Yes.

Bike hire: Yes.

Police station: No.

Restaurants: A limited selection; mainly Greek with some Italian influence.

Tavernas: The provision here is blurred between restaurant and taverna. Some traditional establishments.

Nightclubs/discos: No.

Atmosphere: Quiet, sleepy and relatively sophisticated. A bigger emphasis on diving and exploration than the more usual beach holiday. A very small resort with masses of "real Greece" appeal.

Drinking water: Drink bottled.

Interruptions to electricity supply: Yes!

Torch needed: Yes.

Cinema: No.

Golf course: No.

Resort environment: A small community set between hills and gathered around an exquisite bay, with the lovely island of Marathonissi seemingly capable of being touched as it sits beckoningly in the bay. Green trees are everywhere, herb-carpeted olive groves and even an interesting old hill village are close by to explore.

Nearest beach: Resort. 0 - 1 km. depending on location of accommodation. Diving Centre.

Ferries: Local trip boats to Marathonissi and the nearby sea caves. Nearest ferry is the link to mainland Killini from Zakynthos Town.
Distance from airport: About 18 km.
Boat mooring: There is a harbour but it's normally occupied by commercial craft. An alternative is to moor off in the spectacular bay.
Any other comments: Tranquility, fresh herbs and wonderful food, a beautiful bay and lots to explore close by. This is the Zakynthos of previous years and hopefully it won't change.

Laganas Λαγανάς   L

Resort location/description: An enormous resort now spreading over a very wide area and overpowering the beautiful Laganas Bay. The main road from Zakynthos Town to Keri brings you here and, once you make the left turn to the resort, you are almost immediately immersed into 3 km. of neon and glitter "strip" that just gets worse and worse as you journey onwards. Its tentacles now extend into the surrounding village areas and it is also growing down the road towards Kalamaki too. You will be excused if you fail to recognise that you are in Greece at all.
Taxis/public transport: Buses and taxis are plentiful
Banks and cash machines: Yes, plus ATM cash machines.
Currency exchange: Hotels, supermarkets, tourist offices and a host of others will all happily exchange your money.
Hotels and accommodation: Large hotels, apartment complexes and more humble self catering accommodation. Most is pre-let to package companies.
Shops: A wide selection although there is still an emphasis on tourist requisites.
Supermarkets: Yes. Mainly mini-markets. For large supermarkets you need to travel to the outskirts of Zakynthos Town
Chemist/pharmacy: Yes.
Disabled friendly: Yes. Laganas is a flat resort with wheelchair access extending to the beach in several places and pedestrian only areas at night.
Doctors/medical centre: Yes.
Petrol station: Yes, located in the resort and on the main Zakynthos road.
Car hire: Yes.
Bike hire: Motor bikes and pedal cycles.

Police station: No. Frequent patrols day and night.

Restaurants: Indian, Chinese, Tex-Mex, McDonalds - even some Greek restaurants.

Tavernas: Lots but you're unlikely to find an authentic one.

Nightclubs/discos: Yes. Several. Additionally, there is a range of music bars.

Atmosphere: Late to bed late to rise, young (no, very young), party - party, beach resort. Loud, brash and with little to commend it beyond the widest selection of entertainment on the island.

Drinking water: Use bottled except in hotels.

Interruptions to electricity supply: Infrequent.

Torch needed: No.

Cinema: Alas, no longer. Music bars tend to show current offerings along with Sky Sports and Karaoke events.

Golf course: No.

Resort environment: A concrete and neon glitter city. Come here to meet ten thousand other tourists and party. Don't come if you're after seclusion or even your own space on the beach.

Nearest beach: Resort. 0 - 1 km. depending on the location of your accommodation.

Ferries: Nearest is Zakynthos Town to mainland Killini - 10 km. away.

Distance from airport: 5 km.

Boat mooring: There is a small harbour close to the islet of Ag. Sostis near the main resort. Mooring opportunities here are strictly limited.

Any other comments: If your holiday is incomplete without a "bucking bronco" ride, you'll probably enjoy it here. Come here to meet people, not to get away from them.

Lithakia
Λιθακιά

Resort location/description: Follow the Keri road from Zakynthos Town, past the turning for Laganas and onwards through small villages for several kilometres before arriving at the crossroads village of Lithakia. The resort area is accessed by taking a left turn at the crossroads and then onwards through the olive groves until the coast is reached. Ten years ago, this was nothing more than an overspill cluster of tavernas catering for those who preferred to walk out of Laganas rather than into it. Now however it's a chic little resort with beachside tavernas providing a focus and a selection of small hotels and self catering accommodation available close by.

Taxis/public transport: Telephone a taxi. Buses serve the main village but that's it.

Banks and cash machines: No.

Currency exchange: Shops and the tourist office will oblige.

Hotels and accommodation: A few small hotels and some self catering accommodation.

Shops: Strictly limited.

Supermarkets: One or two smaller mini-markets.

Chemist/pharmacy: No. The nearest is at Laganas.

Disabled friendly: The resort is relatively flat but, disappointingly, all access points to the beach involve steps.

Doctors/medical centre: No. The nearest is at Laganas.

Petrol station: In the centre of the main village.

Car hire: Yes.

Bike hire: Motor bikes, cycles and even boats for hire.

Police station: No.

Restaurants: A fair selection of mainly Greek and Italian influence plus fast food and cafe bars.

Tavernas: Somewhat blurred between restaurant and taverna in the resort. For an authentic village taverna, try the main village.

Nightclubs/discos: No.

Atmosphere: Considering its proximity to Laganas, Lithakia is considerably lower key and provides a pleasant respite from the heaving multitudes associated with that resort. Come here to eat, sleep, swim and relax.

Drinking water: Drink bottled.

Interruptions to electricity supply: Occasional.

Torch needed: Advisable.

Cinema: No. One or two of the bars show current films.

Golf course: No.

Resort environment: This is an attractive, if somewhat artificial, resort. The sea front's wooden promenade with its fish taverna balconies is unique on Zakynthos. What it lacks in facilities it makes up for in atmosphere.

Nearest beach: Resort. 0 - 1 km. depending on the location of your accommodation.

Ferries: Nearest link is Zakynthos Town to mainland Killini.

Distance from airport: 15 km.

Boat mooring: No.

Any other comments: Lithakia is all about placid, relaxing beach holidays. There is some limited night life but it's sufficiently close to Laganas to walk if the desire to boogie on down takes you. Come here to escape from crowds rather than to discover them.

Tsilivi *Τσιλιβή*   t

Resort location/description: A rapidly growing, sprawling resort that takes in neighbouring Planos and Bouka. Until recently had a policy of keeping space between all of its facilities. This seems to now be sacrificed in favour of maximising profit opportunities. Located on the east coast, in the middle of the island and surrounded by olive groves and grapes. This has traditionally been a family resort with a significant emphasis on its wide, golden beach.

Taxis/public transport: Bus service and taxis prowl the resort.

Banks and cash machines: There is now an ATM cash machine cluster on the main road through the resort. For a bank, you need to go to the main town.

Currency exchange: Lots of exchange facilities in hotels, supermarkets, travel offices etc.

Hotels and accommodation: A wide selection of low rise hotels ranging in standard, including one or two of the most exclusive ones on the island. Self catering accommodation is also plentiful. Much of the accommodation is pre-let to tour companies. You will normally find somewhere to stay, although you may find more success at the periphery of the resort or just outside it, in August.

Shops: The usual range of tourist orientated offerings.

Supermarkets: One or two quite large supermarkets and a range of mini-markets located throughout the resort.

Chemist/pharmacy: Yes.

Disabled friendly: Yes. This is a fairly flat resort with wheelchair access routinely available to the beach.

Doctors/medical centre: Yes.

Petrol station: Yes. In the village itself and on the main roads leading to the resort.

Car hire: Yes.

Bike hire: Motor bikes and pedal cycles for hire.

Police station: No.

Restaurants: A wide selection; mainly Greek or Italian in emphasis. There are also Chinese, fast-food and cafe bars along with the ubiquitous souvlaki shops.

Tavernas: Mainly tourist orientated. Travel to the nearby inland villages for the real thing.

Nightclubs/discos: One or two nightclubs. Main provision is music bars which stay open quite late.

Atmosphere: Beach orientated, family resort. Laid back, but sufficiently large that there's nearly always something going on. Lots of facilities and lots of people - though you don't notice this quite as much as the resort spreads over such a wide area.

Drinking water: Drink bottled except in hotels.

Interruptions to electricity supply: Occasional.

Torch needed: No. Unless your accommodation is located in the olive groves when one may come in useful.

Cinema: No. Many of the bars show films or have Sky Movies or Sport channel on offer.

Golf course: No.

Resort environment: Spacious, sprawling and possessing many faces. It covers a wide area with incongruous concrete and neon sprinkled through the pretty olive groves. Good family resort catering more for the twenty to forty age group.

Nearest beach: Resort. For an alternative, travel five km. to nearby Ampoula.

Ferries: From Zakynthos Town to mainland Killini.

Distance from airport: About 20 km.

Boat mooring: No.

Any other comments: Now possesses a maritime museum! One or two horse riding ranches. Having managed to keep space between its facilities until recently, hopefully it has not made the mistake that Laganas has, allowing uncontrolled expansion of low grade facilities. Spectacular beach with good facilities. Pleasant walks and excursions close by.

zakynthos

beaches

ZAKYNTHOSbeaches

Aghia Kiriaki *Αγία Κυριακή*

$\frac{175}{250}$ ★★★★

Beach location: From the main crossroads at Alykanas, follow the signs for the beach. You will come to a T junction where you turn left, proceeding through the olive groves for about 0.5 km. and Ag. Kiriaki beach is then reached.

Disabled access: There are steps in places but some points at which a wheelchair can access the beach.

Car parking: Park on the roadside where there's plenty of space.

Food outlets/restaurants: A taverna, a beach bar and a shop.

Sand/pebbles/shingle: Golden sand into a placid, shallow bay.
Sunbeds/umbrellas: Yes.
Showers: No.
Safe for children: The sea here is gentle and stays shallow for some distance. There's sometimes incoming weed at high water.
Watersports: No.
Main users: Tourists.
Well cared for: Comparatively but spoiled by litter.
Mooring for boats: A small harbour is usually full of small fishing boats and local leisure craft.
Next to quayside/harbour: This is not obtrusive.
Storm drains/outlets into sea: None observed.
Natural shady areas: The beach is very exposed and it can be windy.
Any other facilities: Alykanas is about 1 km. with more extensive facilities.
Distance to main resorts: Alykanas 1 km. Alykes 4 km.
Public transport: Bus service to Alykanas Village. Otherwise phone a taxi.
Blue Flag: No.

145
250

Aghios Nikolaos
Άγιος Νικόλαος

Beach location: Not to be confused with the Aghios Nikolaos Beach to the south of the island, on the Vassilikos Peninsula, this Ag. Nikolaos is located far to the north. Proceed (with caution) through Volimes Village (where

eSCAPE to tHE...beaches

the locals will jump on your car and force you to buy a pot of honey or a rug!). Then follow the signs for Skinari, Ag. Nikolaos or the Cephalonia Ferry. The road loops around to bring you into the harbour and beach area.

Disabled access: There is a steep ramp, but it's just about possible to get a wheelchair down.

Car parking: There is now extensive parking associated with the massive new ferry terminal. Otherwise, park on the roadside or adjacent to the tavernas.

a

eSCAPE tO tHE.. beaches

Food outlets/restaurants: Yes. This is becoming a min-resort, mainly because of the proximity of the Cephalonia Ferry.
Sand/pebbles/shingle: Shale and pebble to and beyond the waterline.
Sunbeds/umbrellas: Sunbeds only.
Showers: No.
Safe for children: While the sea is calm most of the time, there are significant boat movements to contend with.

Watersports: No. The best you'll get (in fact the only thing you'll get) is a boat trip to the Blue Caves.

Main users: Tourists and locals.

Well cared for: No.

Mooring for boats: Yes. Use the extensive harbour or, if you don't like concrete monstrosities, moor off in the pretty bay.

Next to quayside/harbour: Yes. Some signs of oil and distinctly unattractive.

Storm drains/outlets into sea: None observed.

Natural shady areas: Yes. Trees to the waterline.

Any other facilities: An embryonic resort. Shops, accommodation, petrol station and restaurants.

Distance to main resorts: 40 km. Zakynthos Town. 20 km. Alykes.

Public transport: Infrequent buses or telephone a taxi.

Blue Flag: No.

a

Aghios Nikolaos (Vasilikos)
Άγιος Νικόλαος(Βασιλικός)

$\frac{205}{250}$

Beach location: Take the Vassilikos Road from Argassi, about 4km beyond the main town. Follow this for about 12km. It is difficult to miss

54

the massive, road-side sign boards that point you left, down a winding road via peasant cottages, goats and even peacocks, bringing you into a small hamlet area and the two beaches associated with St. Nicholas Bay.

Disabled access: St Nicholas, and most of the surrounding area, is relatively flat. Although there are few specific attempts made to accommodate disabled visitors, the area is fairly accessible for wheelchairs.

Car parking: This beach is undoubtedly the busiest on the peninsula - if not

eSCAPE tO tHE... beaches

on the island - and is heavily marketed (and used). It gets very busy and you may find yourself having to park beyond the car parks, on the roadside itself. There is normally space.

Food outlets/restaurants: Beach bars and tavernas complete with day

time "chill-out" disco music!
Sand/pebbles/shingle: Beautiful golden sand (if you can see it for bodies) extending into a lovely, sweeping blue bay; rocky outcrops and a small family church on the headland.

Sunbeds/umbrellas: Yes. Hundreds!

Showers: Yes. Toilets care of the owners of local facilities.

Safe for children: Yes. This is a shallow bay and quite safe for less confident swimmers. Bear in mind watersports activity and also that it gets incredibly busy in the high season.

Watersports: Yes.

Main users: Tourists.

Well cared for: Yes.

Mooring for boats: No.

Next to quayside/harbour: No.

Storm drains/outlets into sea: None observed.

Natural shady areas: No. The beach is entirely exposed.

Any other facilities: A tourist village is springing up to the rear of the main hotel complex.

Distance to main resorts: 12km. from Argassi. 15km. from Zakynthos.

Public transport: The public bus will get you only as far as the main road and it's a significant walk from there. There is a well advertised private bus that picks up tourists at the main resorts and drops them here for the day, collecting them later. Otherwise, it's a taxi or independent transport.

Blue Flag: No.

eSCAPE eSCAPE tO tHE...beaches a

165
250 ★★★★★

Aghios Sostis
Άγιος Σώστης

Beach location: From Laganas resort, take the secondary road towards Lithakia and follow the signs for the "Cameo" Disco. If you're proposing to walk, fix your view on the small islet at the eastern end of the main Laganas beach, with a small harbour adjacent. The islet is Ag. Sostis. To

reach the beach you must traverse the somewhat rickety wooden causeway leading to the islet. Then climb the steps and walk the path beyond the main bar/disco area to reach the beach.

Disabled access: No. The causeway is of relatively ramshackle construction and there are countless steps both up to the islet and down to the beach.

Car parking: Park in the harbour area.

Food outlets/restaurants: There are snack facilities on the islet and tavernas close to the harbour and in nearby Lithakia.

a

eSCAPE tO tHE... beaches

eSCAPE tO tHE beaches

Sand/pebbles/shingle: The beach comprises large pebbles with a liberal sprinkling of sea urchins.

Sunbeds/umbrellas: Yes.

Showers: No.

Safe for children: This is an exciting but potentially dangerous environment and children will need supervision. Footwear, as protection from the sea urchins, is advisable.

Watersports: No.

Main users: Tourists by day, locals (at least in the disco) at night.

Well cared for: Could be a lot better.

beaches

Mooring for boats: Moor in the harbour adjacent. Space is very limited.
Next to quayside/harbour: The harbour is unobtrusive.
Storm drains/outlets into sea: No.
Natural shady areas: There is a garden area with shading trees.
Any other facilities: Rooms to let, mini-markets and other resort facilities within a few hundred metres.
Distance to main resorts: 1km. Laganas - less than that from Lithakia.
Public transport: A bus will take you within 1 km. Otherwise, taxi or independent transport is required.
Blue Flag: No.

180
250 ★★★★ GOLD

Alykanas
Αλικανάς

Beach location: From the main road junction at Alykanas, follow the beach signs-proceeding beyond the turning for Ag. Kiriaki, until the beach is reached.

Disabled access: Very limited. There are small steps to the beach in most places, with one or two access points suitable for wheelchairs. An alternative is to sojourn in the pleasant gardens of the Alykanas Beach Hotel which is wheelchair accessible and open to the public.

Car parking: There is little specific parking provision. The alternatives are to park in a taverna or hotel car park or, otherwise, park on the roadside.

Food outlets/restaurants: One or two beach or snack bars with lots more provision in the main resort area.

Sand/pebbles/shingle: Golden sand and a sprinkling of small pebbles, at and beyond the waterline.

Sunbeds/umbrellas: Yes.

Showers: The local hotel provides a courtesy shower.

Safe for children: The sea is relatively safe but it can get windy here, whipping the water up.

Watersports: Limited provision. Canoes, pedaloes, jet skis and windsurfing.

Main users: Tourists.

Well cared for: Spoiled a little by litter.

Mooring for boats: A small harbour is located close by but places here are very limited.

Next to quayside/harbour: No.

Storm drains/outlets into sea: None observed.

Natural shady areas: The beach is entirely open to the sea and it can be windy.

Any other facilities: Full resort facilities close by.

Distance to main resorts: 0 - 1 km. Alykanas.

Public transport: Buses as far as the village. Otherwise, phone for a taxi.

Blue Flag: No.

195
250

★ ★ ★ ★ GOLD

Alykes
Αλυκές

Beach location: Follow the north-east coastal route from Zakynthos Town to the resort of Alykes, about twenty kilometres north. Once in the resort, you turn right from one of several access points to reach the beach and river area.
Disabled access: Yes. This is a flat resort with beach access perfectly

possible for wheelchairs.

Car parking: There's a parking area for about twenty cars or park on the roadside, where possible.

Food outlets/restaurants: Yes-a large selection, although not much on the beach itself.

Sand/pebbles/shingle: Golden sand with a light sprinkling of small pebbles.

Sunbeds/umbrellas: Yes.

Showers: Yes.

Safe for children: Yes. This is a pleasant resort beach with placid, shallow

waters.
Watersports: Yes.
Main users: Tourists.
Well cared for: Comparatively. Could do better.
Mooring for boats: There's a harbour between Alykes and Alykanas.
Next to quayside/harbour: No. Some boats moor in the mouth of the river but they're unobtrusive.

Storm drains/outlets into sea: None observed.
Natural shady areas: No. The beach is very exposed.
Any other facilities: Full resort facilities.
Distance to main resorts: 0 to 1 km. depending on the location of your accommodation.
Public transport: Bus service and plentiful taxis.
Blue Flag: No.

a

eSCAPE to tHE... beaches

165
250 ★★★★

Amoudi
Αμμούδι

Beach location: From the Zakynthos to Alykes road, watch out for the signposted right turn which leads you to this beach. Alternately, follow the directions for Shoestring Beach from Alykanas, proceeding beyond that beach and taking the coast road until Amoudi is reached.

Disabled access: Strictly limited. There's a steep slope and a rocky track down to the hard sand beach but it should be accessible for wheelchairs, with caution.

Car parking: There are two or three car parks associated with local tavernas where you can park.

Food outlets/restaurants: There are several beach bars and restaurants behind the beach.

Sand/pebbles/shingle: Rocky approaches lead to a golden sand, strip beach with small pebbles beyond the waterline in places.

Sunbeds/umbrellas: Yes.

Showers: No.

Safe for children: This is a relatively placid seascape. However it can get windy. Beyond this, the water goes deep in places and there are submerged rocks to beware of.

Watersports: No.
Main users: Tourists and locals.
Well cared for: While this is still a pleasant beach, it would benefit from more attention to litter and weed which tends to float in with the tide.
Mooring for boats: No.
Next to quayside/harbour: No.
Storm drains/outlets into sea: No.
Natural shady areas: Green cliffs behind the beach give a little respite, but not much.
Any other facilities: A tiny resort is springing up behind the beach.
Distance to main resorts: Zakynthos Town is 15 km. Alykes/Alykanas are both 5km. away.
Public transport: No.
Blue Flag: No.

a

beaches

eSCAPE to the... beaches

Ampoula (Amboula) Αμπουλα

$\frac{180}{250}$ ★★★★ GOLD

Beach location: Next door to the large Louis Pelagos Beach Hotel, which is a useful landmark. Take the Zakynthos to Alykes coastal road. The beach is located close by Kipselli and Tsilivi, and is signposted from both. The road gives out at the beach.

Disabled access: There is a steep ramp to the beach and garden area.

Car parking: About twenty cars will fit in the parking area. Otherwise, park on the roadway.

Food outlets/restaurants: There are three or four tavernas and snack bars.

Sand/pebbles/shingle: Golden sand with some pebbles in places.

Sunbeds/umbrellas: Yes.

Showers: Yes.

Safe for children: This is open sea with waves and quite a swell. The water gets deep quite quickly.

Watersports: No.

Main users: A mixture of locals and tourists.

Well cared for: Could be better (and certainly has been in the past).

Mooring for boats: No.

Next to quayside/harbour: No.

Storm drains/outlets into sea: None observed.
Natural shady areas: No, the beach is exposed.
Any other facilities: Rooms to let and a mini-market.
Distance to main resorts: Zakynthos is about 15 km. Tsilivi is 5 km.
Public transport: No.
Blue Flag: No (although it used to have one some years ago).

eSCAPE eSCAPE tO tHE...beaches a

eSCAPE tO tHE... beaches

Argassi (Argasi)
Αργάσι

$\frac{180}{250}$ ★★★☆☆ GOLD

Beach location: From Zakynthos Town, take the Vassilikos road, over the river and then left and, bearing right, follow the winding road until you rejoin the coast. You then travel for about four km. without deviating and

this brings you into Argassi. On reaching the centre of Argassi, the beach is accessed on the left hand side, at a number of points.

Disabled access: Wheelchair access is available at only one or two points.

Car parking: This is a nightmare! Park wherever you can on the main road in the resort and walk.

Food outlets/restaurants: Lots, including beach bars and loads of tavernas.

Sand/pebbles/shingle: The narrowest of strip beaches with soft sand and

some small pebbles in places. Far from attractive!

Sunbeds/umbrellas: Yes.

Showers: Yes. Care of tavernas and hotels.

Safe for children: Relatively safe. However, there are watersports operating and open seas beyond. The narrow strip makes it difficult to keep youngsters in view. Supervision is required.

Watersports: Yes.

Main users: Tourists.

Well cared for: The beach is cleaned and weed removed regularly but it does little to improve it. Needs a major facelift!

Mooring for boats: No.
Next to quayside/harbour: No.
Storm drains/outlets into sea: Yes.
Natural shady areas: Some tree cover and a pleasant garden with umbrellas close to the area of the Castello Beach Hotel, at the centre of the beach.
Any other facilities: Full resort facilities available.
Distance to main resorts: 0 - 1 km. depending on location of your accommodation.
Public transport: Buses and taxis serve the resort.
Blue Flag: No.

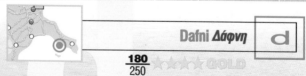

Dafni *Δάφνη*   d

$\dfrac{180}{250}$ ★★★★ GOLD

Beach location: Dafni is one of only a couple of beaches on the Vassilikos Peninsula that is accessed from the right hand side of the road. It's about 10 km. from Argassi along the peninsula road and you need to keep a look out for unofficial signs pointing to the beach. Having turned right, the road

is initially surfaced but soon gives out into a boulder strewn, dirt track. This you must take very slowly and your car will get very, very dusty. Dafni is centred in a large bay overlooking the tiny islet of Pelouzon.

Disabled access: It's just about possible to get a wheelchair onto the beach in places.

Car parking: Yes. Park adjacent to the taverna areas.

Food outlets/restaurants: There are two tavernas and two beach bars.

Sand/pebbles/shingle: This is golden sand with some large pebbles. It gives out into pure sand (and a fair amount of weed) beyond the water-line. A rugged beach with relative tranquillity.

Sunbeds/umbrellas: Yes. Limited provision.

Showers: Yes.

Safe for children: The water here is very placid. The sea shelves gently and it's quite shallow initially. Suitable for novice swimmers.

Watersports: No.

Main users: Locals, with an increasing number of tourists now it's been opened up a bit.

Well cared for: Since finding tourism, Dafni has started to suffer from litter and uncleared weed.

Mooring for boats: No.
Next to quayside/harbour: No.
Storm drains/outlets into sea: No.
Natural shady areas: There are some trees around the taverna areas giving respite from the heat. The beach itself is exposed.
Any other facilities: No.
Distance to main resorts: 10 km. Argassi. 15 km. Zakynthos Town.
Public transport: No.
Blue Flag: No.

200 / 250

Drossia
Δροσιά

Beach location: You are likely to get lost! Drossia is located beyond the Gerakari villages on Zakynthos' north-east coast, hidden behind a maze of

back roads that meander between the villages and the coast. It's about 1 km. from Kipselli Village and close to the Belousi Apartments. Both the beach and the apartments are unofficially signposted from the road.

Disabled access: Although the track is relatively steep, wheelchair access is possible at several points along the beach.

Car parking: The car park is associated with the apartment complex (where, if you prefer, you can use the pool). Alternately, park on the road.

Food outlets/restaurants: Two or three tavernas and snack bars.
Sand/pebbles/shingle: Part sand - part pebble, a series of narrow strips separated by breakwaters.
Sunbeds/umbrellas: Yes.
Showers: Yes.
Safe for children: Beware of rocks hidden under the water. Although the water is normally placid, wind and waves can be present at certain times.
Watersports: No.

Main users: Used by a mixture of tourists and locals.
Well cared for: Yes, in the main.
Mooring for boats: No.
Next to quayside/harbour: No.
Storm drains/outlets into sea: No.
Natural shady areas: Small cliffs behind the beach afford no real protection from the sun.
Any other facilities: Rooms, one or two shops and a taverna or two are located close by.
Distance to main resorts: Zakynthos Town is about 12 km. to the south.
Public transport: No.
Blue Flag: No.

eSCAPE tO tHE... beaches

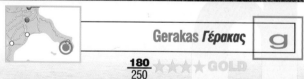

Gerakas *Γέρακας* | g

$\frac{180}{250}$ ★★★★ GOLD

Beach location: Take the winding road from Argassi, 4 kilometres beyond Zakynthos Town, and follow it down the splendid Vassilikos Peninsula until - after about 17 kilometres - you come to a minor crossroads. Straight over takes you to Gerakas. You will have to park in the impromptu car park (field!) and descend down the cliffside on foot. It is not until you are able to gaze out from the hillside at the spectacular vista unfold-

ing below and around you that you will appreciate what a wise choice you have made in coming.

Disabled access: No. There is a steep, unmade pathway down to the beach and (occasional) storms have left deep gouges in the clay. This conspires to make wheelchair access extremely difficult if not impossible.

Car parking: The unofficial car park will take up to 100 cars. However, it does get very full and you may have to resort to roadside parking.

Food outlets/restaurants: Nothing on the beach itself as this is a protected area. Cantina vans have come and gone over the years but are unlikely to re-emerge. There is a small selection of tavernas set back on the roadside close to the beach.

Sand/pebbles/shingle: Gerakas possesses beautiful, soft gold sand and

eSCAPE tO tHE... beaches

eSCAPE tO tHE... beaches

is surrounded by needle-like cliffs. You will have difficulty finding a pebble!
Sunbeds/umbrellas: Yes.
Showers: No. For toilets you must rely on the tavernas or the sea!

Safe for children: This is a shallow bay and eminently suitable for youngsters. More adventurous swimmers and those with mask and flippers will find the surrounding area well worthy of exploration.

Watersports: No.

Main users: Apart from the Loggerhead turtles that visit in the summer, this is a major day-trip tourist beach and can get busy though seldom overcrowded. The beach closes at 7 p.m. when the night shift (in the shape of the turtles) takes over!

Well cared for: Yes.

Mooring for boats: Some yachts moor off for a (well worthwhile) visit. There is no real shelter, however and the bay is relatively shallow.

Next to quayside/harbour: No.

Storm drains/outlets into sea: No.

Natural shady areas: The spiky, clay cliffs provide a little cover and there is some scrubby vegetation in places. Substantially, however, the area is open to the elements.

Any other facilities: A mini-market, a few rooms to let and a couple more eateries and shops in the neighbouring beach harbour of Porto Roma is about all that there is. A Sea Turtle Protection Society kiosk hands out useful information on the turtles and there is a small photographic exhibition.

Distance to main resorts: Zakynthos Town is 20km. Argassi about 17km.

Public transport: Occasional bus service (to Porto Roma). Otherwise, phone a taxi or utilise independent transport. Bicycles are not recommended as the Vassilikos Peninsula is quite hilly.

Blue Flag: No. (It is incomprehensible why not).

Ionian Beach Ιόνιον

185/250 ★★★★ GOLD

Beach location: This is another of the non-resort beaches located along the Vassilikos Peninsula - approached from the main road through Argassi. It's a continuation of the coastline, located before Spianza (Banana) and is signposted on the left hand side of the main road.

Disabled access: Although theoretically possible, there are steep tracks to the beach and, depending on your attempted point of access, wheelchair users may find it extremely difficult.

Car parking: Car parking for thirty to forty cars. This usually copes with the daily influx of visitors.

Food outlets/restaurants: Yes. There's a small selection of beach bars and tavernas.

Sand/pebbles/shingle: Golden sand giving out into pebbles at and beyond

the waterline.

Sunbeds/umbrellas: Yes.

Showers: Yes. For toilets, use bars or tavernas.

Safe for children: The sea gets deep quickly. The currents are fast and there is quite a swell with significant waves. This is open sea with tidal sand spits. Young swimmers will require supervision.

Watersports: No.

Main users: Tourists and locals.

Well cared for: Yes.

Mooring for boats: No.

Next to quayside/harbour: No.

Storm drains/outlets into sea: No.

Natural shady areas: No. This is an exposed and windy coastline.

Any other facilities: Rooms to let close by.

Distance to main resorts: Zakynthos is about 10km. Argassi is 6 km.

Public transport: Only to the main road, about 1km away. Independent transport or a taxi required.

Blue Flag: No.

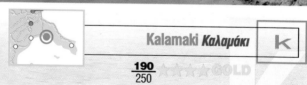

Kalamaki *Καλαμάκι* | k

$\frac{190}{250}$ ★★★☆☆ GOLD

Beach location: From the main Zakynthos to Laganas road, follow the signs for Kalamaki, through the resort and on towards the beach itself. Alternately, there is a road from Laganas running parallel to the beach and

eSCAPE to tHE... beaches

adjacent to the airport. Turn right at the end of that road, through the resort and the beach is a couple of hundred metres.

Disabled access: No. There are steep drops to the beach via cliff tracks.

Car parking: Yes but it's limited. There's probably space for about thirty to forty cars at the top of the cliff and some space on the roadside itself. Parking in the resort is very limited.

Food outlets/restaurants: Very little (in fact none) on the beach. Plenty reasonably close by.

Sand/pebbles/shingle: Rich golden sand.

Sunbeds/umbrellas: Yes.

eSCAPE tO tHE beaches

eSCAPE tO tHE.. beaches

Showers: No.
Safe for children: This is calm, shallow sea - ideal for younger swimmers.
Turtle spotting trips are organised.
Watersports: No.
Main users: Tourists.
Well cared for: Yes.
Mooring for boats: No.
Next to quayside/harbour: No.
Storm drains/outlets into sea: None observed.

beaches

Natural shady areas: No. This beach is relatively exposed - albeit there are some sand dunes.
Any other facilities: A full range of resort facilities close by.
Distance to main resorts: 0 - 2 km. depending on the location of your accommodation. Kalamaki is spreading along the bay towards Laganas. The closer to Laganas, the flatter and more wheelchair friendly.
Public transport: Buses call occasionally and taxis prowl in the area of the resort.
Blue Flag: No.

eSCAPE eSCAPE tO tHE... beaches

Kaminia
Καμίνια

195
250 ★ ★ ★ ★ GOLD

Beach location: A good, if somewhat steep, surfaced road leads to Kaminia between Argassi and Vassilikos. It's about 6km. beyond Argassi itself. You need to be prepared to turn quickly as the sign comes up suddenly on the left hand side of the road. And then it's down the steep track to the tree lined bay beyond.

Disabled access: Yes. Wheelchairs can get onto the beach itself, although you'll need to arrive by car as that steep track down is something else!

Car parking: Yes. There are substantial parking places at the beach itself. Parking only becomes a difficulty in August.

Food outlets/restaurants: There are two tavernas that double as beach bars.

Sand/pebbles/shingle: This is a fine shingle mingled with golden sand beach. There are pebbles beyond the waterline.

Sunbeds/umbrellas: Yes.

Showers: Yes.

Safe for children: There are strong tides and waves. Plus the water gets deep quite quickly. Supervise less proficient swimmers.

Watersports: No.
Main users: Used by locals and tourists.
Well cared for: Yes.
Mooring for boats: No.
Next to quayside/harbour: No.
Storm drains/outlets into sea: No.
Natural shady areas: Yes. There are trees behind the beach and a pleas-

ant garden area that's a nice diversion if the heat on the sand gets too much.

Any other facilities: Rooms to let and a mini-market on the main road.

Distance to main resorts: Argassi 6 km. Zakynthos 10 km.

Public transport: You can catch the Vassilikos bus to the main road and then walk. Otherwise, a taxi or independent transport is required.

Blue Flag: No.

eSCAPE tO tHE... beaches

185 / 250 ★★★ GOLD **Keri** *Κερί*

Beach location: A good road leads from Zakynthos Town to Keri, albeit it's twisty in parts. As you approach Keri, take the lower road signposted to Keri Port (Limni Keriou). The higher road takes you to pleasant Keri Village but as this is located half way up a mountain, you won't see much of the sea!

Disabled access: Wheelchair access is available to most areas of Keri. The beach itself has a limited number of access points and you can park close by, on the roadside.

Car parking: There's a significant parking area at the harbour, plus some facilities adjacent to tavernas as well as on the roadside.

Food outlets/restaurants: A reasonable selection.

Sand/pebbles/shingle: Large pebbles to and beyond the waterline with a few sandy areas.

Sunbeds/umbrellas: Yes.

eSCAPE eSCAPE tO tHE... beaches

Showers: Yes. Although you'll be charged the grand sum of 1 euro for the privilege!

Safe for children: The sea is normally quite placid although it can get windy with occasional waves as a consequence.

Watersports: Very limited. Boat hire, pedaloes and canoes along with diving tuition.

Main users: Used both by tourists and locals.

Well cared for: Yes.

Mooring for boats: Moor in the commercial harbour if there is space available.
Next to quayside/harbour: This is unobtrusive.
Storm drains/outlets into sea: Yes. Storm drains.
Natural shady areas: Some trees close to the waterline provide shelter.
Any other facilities: Rooms, shops eateries and most facilities you'll require.
Distance to main resorts: 20 km. Zakynthos Town.
Public transport: Bus service or phone for a taxi.
Blue Flag: No.

eSCAPE tO tHE... beaches
eSCAPE tO tHE beaches
eSCAPE

 155 ★★★★ beachname **Krioneri**
250 *Κρυονέρι*

Beach location: Follow the harbour road from the port in Zakynthos Town in the direction of Akrotiri. The beach is located about 1 km. along the road on the right hand side. This is the town (pay) beach with organised facilities (of sorts). A free provision (the Asteria Plaz - associated with a beachside taverna - is located next door).

Disabled access: Only as far as the garden area (which is more attractive than the scrappy beach anyway).

Car parking: On the road adjacent to the complex.

Food outlets/restaurants: There are two or three snack bars or tavernas adjacent to the complex.

Sand/pebbles/shingle: The beach is pebble and shingle, to and beyond the waterline.

Sunbeds/umbrellas: Yes.

Showers: Yes.

Safe for children: This is open sea with fast water, waves and a swell that is exacerbated by passing ferries. It gets deep quite quickly and is unat-

beaches

tractive. Playing in the adjacent swing park and sports area is probably a more interesting proposition!

Watersports: No.

Main users: Locals (who must be desperate or very short of time!)

Well cared for: No. The whole area has gone down over the years and now presents a seedy, down at heel atmosphere. And you have to pay for the privilege! Look elsewhere.

Mooring for boats: No. Zakynthos Harbour is approximately 1 km.

Next to quayside/harbour: No.

Storm drains/outlets into sea: None observed.

Natural shady areas: No.

Any other facilities: Rooms, tavernas and mini-markets relatively close by.

Distance to main resorts: 1 km. Zakynthos Town.

Public transport: Yes. Buses and taxis.

Blue Flag: Yes (absolutely unbelievably!).

eSCAPE tO tHE... beaches

Laganas (Lagana) Λαγανάς　　L

205
250 ★★★★★

Beach location: The main road running from Zakynthos Town to Keri leads past the turning for the airport and Kalamaki and on towards Laganas. After about six km. a wide, straight road - signposted on the left hand side - takes you to the resort and beach. As Laganas Bay stretches for some 9km and most of this is accessible beach, you will appreciate that there are many points at which to access the fine sands.

Disabled access: Yes. Laganas is mainly located in a flat area although there are some exceptions to this, mainly near Lithakia. Wheelchairs will routinely cope in most of the beach areas and the area of the resort itself.

Car parking: Difficult. This is particularly the case at the main beach access points. You may have more luck parking at perimeter areas of the beach but will undoubtedly find yourself walking at some point or other.

Food outlets/restaurants: You name it, Laganas has got it!

Sand/pebbles/shingle: 9km of continuous soft, golden sand (it gets a bit tired looking as the season draws to a close) leading from Kalamaki at one end to Lithakia at the other. Occasional weed in places and you may find yourself drowning in excess sun oil spilled by the thousands of tourists who throng the main beach areas. It's still possible to find an isolated spot most

eSCAPE tO tHE.. beaches

of the year - but you'll have to travel quite a few of those 9 km. to reach it!

Sunbeds/umbrellas: Yes.

Showers: Yes. Toilets care of beach bars and tavernas.

Safe for children: Yes. The beach shelves gently into the shallow waters of the wide, blue bay. There are few waves. Watersports outlets have now been restricted because of turtles nesting in the area.

Watersports: Limited to pedaloes and canoes to help with conservation of the Loggerhead turtles, which are Lagana's oldest tourists.

Main users: Tourists - thousands of them!

Well cared for: Yes but the number of visitors takes its toll on the beach.

Mooring for boats: There is a small harbour adjacent to the beach areas,

close to Lithakia and the islet of Ag. Sostis.

Next to quayside/harbour: The harbour is unobtrusive.

Storm drains/outlets into sea: None observed, although it's almost inevitable that there are some - the resort is so developed.

Natural shady areas: No.

Any other facilities: Full resort facilities provide you with whatever you want.

Distance to main resorts: 0 - 3 km. depending on the location of your accommodation.

Public transport: Buses and taxis are plentiful.

Blue Flag: No.

eSCAPE tO tHE... beaches

155
250

★★★★

Lithakia
Λιθακιά

Beach location: You can either walk from Laganas, via the beach and cliff-side track or, if visiting by car, follow the Lithakia signs (or Laganas Camping) through the back of the resort. Alternately, take the main Zakynthos to Keri road and then follow the beach signs when you get to the crossroads (where you turn left) at Lithakia Village itself.

Disabled access: No. Wheelchairs will only make it to the cluster of tavernas that have built balconies overhanging the beach area.
Car parking: Limited to taverna car parks and the roadside.
Food outlets/restaurants: Yes. Plenty.
Sand/pebbles/shingle: Golden sand with a little weed in places. Considerably more tends to arrive after storms.
Sunbeds/umbrellas: Yes.
Showers: No.
Safe for children: Yes. The water is shallow and sandy. The wind can spring up, however, creating waves.

eSCAPE tO+HE beaches

Watersports: No. Provision is limited to boat hire, pedaloes and canoes.
Main users: Tourists and locals.
Well cared for: Yes.
Mooring for boats: No.
Next to quayside/harbour: No.
Storm drains/outlets into sea: Yes. There are storm drain outlets along the beach.

beaches

Natural shady areas: No. Only the promenade taverna balconies fit the bill!

Any other facilities: The resort has limited additional facilities. Trips to "Turtle Island" (Marathonisi) are available.

Distance to main resorts: 0 - 1 km. depending on location of your accommodation.

Public transport: Buses serve the village and there are taxis available by phone.

Blue Flag: No.

eSCAPE tO tHE... beaches

Makris Gialos
Μακρύς Γιαλός

m

195
250
★★★★ GOLD

Beach location: This is a dangerous trip - inasmuch as you have to ven-
ture into the centre of the craft village of Volimes. Here, the locals jump out
in front of your car and virtually lie across the bonnet until you agree to
buy some trinket or piece of local craft work from them! In the centre of
the village (located to the north of the island) turn right at the T junction
and follow the road (signposted) about 7 km. to Makris Gialos.

Disabled access: There is a steep slope to the beach but it's just about possible for a wheelchair.

Car parking: There's one car park that's quite big. Otherwise, you need to park on the roadside.

Food outlets/restaurants: One snack bar and one taverna are available in the immediate vicinity of the beach. More are located close by.

Sand/pebbles/shingle: The beach comprises shingle and small pebbles.

Sunbeds/umbrellas: Yes.

Showers: No.

Safe for children: Relatively. The water gets deep quite quickly and faces out to the open sea.

Watersports: No.

Main users: Tourists and locals.
Well cared for: Yes.
Mooring for boats: Moor off in the bay.
Next to quayside/harbour: No.
Storm drains/outlets into sea: No.

Natural shady areas: This is an exposed beach.
Any other facilities: Rooms to let close by. Boat trips to the Blue Caves.
Distance to main resorts: Volimes 8 km. Zakynthos Town 35 km.
Public transport: No.
Blue Flag: No.

beaches

$\dfrac{180}{250}$

Mavratzis
Μαυράτζης

Beach location: Located on the beautiful Vassilikos Peninsula, Mavratzis is situated just beyond Vassilikos Village. You turn left from the main road approximately 2km. before it gives out at Porto Roma. Alternately, follow

the signs for the massive monstrosity of a hotel that's been built on the hillside (ruining the local ambience for ever). It's about 15km. from Argassi. A long concrete track gives out at the beach itself. This used to be an extremely pretty, isolated bay but this is no longer the case.

Disabled access: No. There are steps and steep slopes rendering this impossible for wheelchairs and very difficult for many others.

Car parking: Car parking is limited to the roadside (unless you manage to park in the hotel grounds) and it's very difficult to turn round. Indeed it's

eSCAPE tO tHE... beaches

best to turn your vehicle as you park and not to get too near to the end of the track as you may, otherwise, have to reverse back for some distance up the hillside.

Food outlets/restaurants: A beach bar and a taverna - both probably associated with the hotel and certainly catering principally for those staying there.

Sand/pebbles/shingle: Golden sand, with slight amounts of weed at the waterline.

Sunbeds/umbrellas: Yes.

Showers: Yes. Plus there are toilets.

Safe for children: The sea is relatively shallow for some distance making this quite attractive for inexperienced swimmers. There is a (zoned) watersports area to watch out for.

Watersports: Yes. There's a water ski school and the usual offerings of pedaloes, jet skis and assorted white knuckle rides.

Main users: Tourists from the hotel next door.

Well cared for: Yes. However, it's spoiled by the approaches with stagnant water and building rubble being two of its less attractive features.

Mooring for boats: No.

Next to quayside/harbour: No.

Storm drains/outlets into sea: Yes. Beyond the stagnant pond, there are overflow pipes from the hotel and a less than attractive looking stream emptying into the sea.

Natural shady areas: The beach is relatively exposed with rocks and vegetation to the side offering some limited shelter.

Any other facilities: Some rooms to let close by. Tennis courts.

Distance to main resorts: 15 km. to Zakynthos Town. 12km. to Argassi.

Public transport: The public bus will only take you as far as the main road. The hotel has a courtesy mini-bus service if you are good at sneaking a ride. Otherwise, it's phone for a taxi or independent transport.

Blue Flag: No.

eSCAPE tO tHE... beaches

 Pachi Ammos *Παχύ Άμμος*

$$\frac{175}{250}$$ ★★★★

Beach location: From the Zakynthos to Volimes road, take the turning towards Alykes and then follow the road for Kipselli. You'll come to a

major crossroads which you go straight over and then follow the signs for the Tsamis/Camelot Hotel. These signs will take you to the beach, which is adjacent to the hotel. The beach is also signposted from Kipselli Village.

Disabled access: Wheelchairs can make it to the rocky shingle patch at one end of the beach (relatively unattractive) or to the garden of the taverna (which is a far more attractive proposition, with its sunbeds and umbrellas).

Car parking: Limited. Park on the (relatively narrow) road.

Food outlets/restaurants: One taverna.

p

eSCAPE tO tHE... beaches

eSCAPE tO tHE eSCAPE tO tHE beaches

Sand/pebbles/shingle: Pebbles, to and beyond the waterline.
Sunbeds/umbrellas: Only in the garden area of the taverna.
Showers: Yes.
Safe for children: There are submerged rocks and stones underfoot. This is tidal open sea with some swell. Children need to be supervised.
Watersports: No.
Main users: Both locals and tourists.
Well cared for: Yes.

Mooring for boats: No.
Next to quayside/harbour: No.
Storm drains/outlets into sea: No.
Natural shady areas: No. The beach is exposed.
Any other facilities: Rooms to let nearby.
Distance to main resorts: Eighteen (long) kilometres south to Zakynthos.
Public transport: No.
Blue Flag: No.

205/250 ★★★★★

Plaka
Πλάκα

Beach location: Located on the Vassilikos Peninsula, beyond St Nicholas Beach. From the main road, watch out for the signs - turning left and then left again to reach two small, rocky bays associated with Plaka. The area is also home to the Golden Bay Complex, which tends to be signposted

from the road. This is also the location for the best of the facilities.

Disabled access: There are a few steps. However, at the Golden Bay end, you can get as far as a pleasant, beach-side garden - complete with sun umbrellas - with a wheelchair.

Car parking: Yes. Large car park can get busy but there's normally space.

Food outlets/restaurants: The beach bar is not always open but there are two or three tavernas.

Sand/pebbles/shingle: Golden sand facing to open sea, with rocky out-crops.

eSCAPE tO tHE...beaches

Sunbeds/umbrellas: Yes.

Showers: Yes. Toilets courtesy of local tavernas or the complex.

Safe for children: This is open sea with wind and waves. The water gets deep quite quickly and there are tidal sand spits to beware of. Rocks surround the beach areas. This is a beach requiring supervision of young children.

Watersports: Yes. These are limited to one bay.

Main users: Tourists.

Well cared for: Yes.

Mooring for boats: No.

Next to quayside/harbour: No.

Storm drains/outlets into sea: None observed.

Natural shady areas: Some vegetation and rocks to the rear of the beach area provide limited shade.

Any other facilities: Incongruous statues on the rocky promontories are undoubtedly supposed to resemble Greek Gods - but look more like garden gnomes! Kiddies' playground and an attractive swimming pool.

Distance to main resorts: 15km. from Zakynthos. 10km. from Argassi.

Public transport: The beach complex lays on a private bus service to bring people here. Otherwise, the public bus would drop you in the village, some way away. Therefore independent transport or a taxi may be preferred.

Blue Flag: No.

155
250
★★★★★

Porto Koukla
Πόρτο Κούκλα

Beach location: Follow the Zakynthos to Keri road beyond the crossroads at Lithakia. Shortly afterwards, turn left where the road is (unofficially) signposted to Porto Koukla. You are almost certain to get lost as you meander through the olive groves. Porto Koukla is positioned just beyond Lithakia and next door to Keri.

Disabled access: No. Steps and slopes make wheelchair access impossible.

Car parking: Yes. There are parking lots associated with the tavernas, or park on the roadside.

Food outlets/restaurants: Several. Some are somewhat sophisticated with swimming pools!

Sand/pebbles/shingle: Soft sand with a fair old sprinkling of weed for good measure.

Sunbeds/umbrellas: Yes.
Showers: No.
Safe for children: Yes. The sea is mild with few waves.
Watersports: No. Canoes and pedaloes are about the limit of local provision.
Main users: Tourists.

Well cared for: Comparatively.
Mooring for boats: No.
Next to quayside/harbour: No.
Storm drains/outlets into sea: No.
Natural shady areas: The beach is located under a cliff but this doesn't really assist much.

Any other facilities: A mini-resort is in the making.
Distance to main resorts: Laganas is about 7 km. Zakynthos Town is about 18 km.
Public transport: No. You will need to phone for a taxi or possess independent transport.
Blue Flag: No.

175
250 ★★★★

Porto Roma
Πόρτο Ρώμα

Beach location: Follow the long tortuous road from Argassi through the spectacular Vassilikos Peninsula until you come to a minor crossroads after about 16 km. Left takes you to Porto Roma, where the road gives out at the low cliffside leading to the beach and small harbour.

Disabled access: A little effort could make this beach disabled accessible but, currently, it would be extremely difficult for a wheelchair. There is a steep, pitted, cliff-side track which gives out completely at the bottom, requiring one to take a deep step of about 6 inches onto the sand itself.

Car parking: Limited car parking in the olive grove adjacent to the taverna is often enough to cope with the daily visitors. Otherwise park on the road where possible and walk.

Food outlets/restaurants: One taverna adjacent to the beach and one beach bar. More in the nearby hamlet of Porto Roma.

Sand/pebbles/shingle: Pebbles and shingle giving out into a sandier environment at the waterline itself.

Sunbeds/umbrellas: Yes. There aren't many, but they're normally enough.

Showers: No.

Safe for children: The coast here is windy and the sea can get choppy with significant currents running. There is limited harbour activity - mainly very small boats and the odd jet-ski exploring from neighbouring Mavratzis. Supervise inexperienced swimmers. Those who enjoy using mask and flippers will appreciate this area.

Watersports: No.

Main users: Those who visit by (small) pleasure craft and a mixture of inquisitive tourists and locals, normally visiting the large fish taverna.

Well cared for: Yes.

eSCAPE tO tHE... beaches

Mooring for boats: Only the tiniest of harbours, accommodating very small boats.

Next to quayside/harbour: The small harbour is unobtrusive and no detriment is caused to the local environment.

Storm drains/outlets into sea: None observed.

Natural shady areas: There are pine and olive trees surrounding the beach area and vegetation on the beach itself.

Any other facilities: The tiniest of village resorts is located close to the beach. This is little more than a couple of shops and eateries, a few rooms to let and a card phone.

Distance to main resorts: Zakynthos Town 20km. Argassi 16km.

Public transport: Very limited bus service. Otherwise, phone a taxi or use independent transport (motorised!).

Blue Flag: No.

eSCAPE tO tHE... beaches

Porto Vromi *Πόρτο Βρώμη*

$\frac{180}{250}$ GOLD

Beach location: Arguably the most difficult beach on Zakynthos to reach. Follow the west spinal route from Zakynthos Town via Kiliomeno. At

Maries Village, you turn left in the village itself and follow the Porto Vromi signs. You can also take the "scenic" route from Keri, proceeding via Agalas, Kiliomeno, Ag. Leon and Maries. The lovely hill road will bring you, eventually, into the dead-end inlet of Porto Vromi, where the tiny beach is located. Trip boats from here will also take you to Smugglers Wreck.

Disabled access: Yes. A ramp suitable for wheelchairs leads to the pebble beach.

Car parking: Very limited. There is but one car park and it's narrow, catering for possibly twenty cars. Roadside parking is not recommended but, in high season, may be all that's available.

Food outlets/restaurants: One cantina dispenses a strictly limited menu.

Sand/pebbles/shingle: Pebbles descending into a crystal clear sea with some sand underfoot beyond the waterline.

Sunbeds/umbrellas: No.

Showers: No.

Safe for children: Relatively. However, there is extensive boat movement and children will need supervision.

Watersports: No. A few pedaloes and boats for hire.

Main users: Tourists.
Well cared for: Yes.
Mooring for boats: It's possible and quite attractive to moor in the bay.
Next to quayside/harbour: The boats are unobtrusive.
Storm drains/outlets into sea: No.
Natural shady areas: None. This is very exposed.
Any other facilities: No. The nearest facilities are at Maries Village some distance away.
Distance to main resorts: Zakynthos Town is 30 km. away. However, it feels like 50 to drive it!
Public transport: No.
Blue Flag: No.

Porto Zoro (Mare) *Πόρτο Ζόρο*

180
250

Beach location: The first of the main cluster of beaches located on the Vassilikos Peninsula. Take the main coastal road from Zakynthos Town,

through Argassi and onwards for about 6 km. The beach is signposted down a steep track (or alternately through an old quarry) on the left-hand side of the road as it leads towards Vassilikos. It's known by both names.

Disabled access: The simple answer would be no (at least in terms of wheelchairs). The intrepid, may discover one or two points where it's just about possible but it's very hard going!

Car parking: There are a couple of places to park. They get very busy and

145

you may find yourself parking on the roadside (with bricks under your wheels at certain points!).

Food outlets/restaurants: There are a couple of beach bars and snackeries.

Sand/pebbles/shingle: This is a very pleasant combination of sand, rocky outcrops, pebbles and even a few offshore islets.

Sunbeds/umbrellas: Yes.

Showers: Yes. Toilets care of the beach bars.

Safe for children: The waters here are relatively placid even though they lead to open sea. There are lots of pebbles and some large rocks to contend with.

Watersports: No. Perhaps there'll be a pedalo or two, perhaps not.

Main users: Tourists and a few locals.

Well cared for: Yes. Although there are parts that look a bit on the scruffy side.

Mooring for boats: No.

Next to quayside/harbour: No.

Storm drains/outlets into sea: No. .

Natural shady areas: Some bushes at the water's edge provide limited shade for a relative few.

Any other facilities: Rooms to rent on the beach.

Distance to main resorts: Argassi is 6km. Zakynthos is about 10 km.

Public transport: You can catch a (very occasional) bus, getting off at the main road sign and then walk. Alternately, phone a taxi or visit using independent transport.

Blue Flag: No.

p

eSCAPE tO tHE... beaches

145 / **250** ★ ★ ★

Psarou
Ψαρού

Beach location: This is a beach that's particularly well hidden! Head for the triumvirate of villages, containing the name Gerakari, on the north-east side of the island. As you drive along the road, you'll see a splendid church on the tree-lined hillside. Use that as your landmark to begin looking for the signs for Psarou. You can also follow the signs for Paradise Camping.

Disabled access: Yes. A slipway style ramp will access wheelchairs to the beach.

Car parking: Park on the roadside where there's space for about thirty cars.

Food outlets/restaurants: There's only one snack bar cum restaurant at the beach although other facilities are located close by.
Sand/pebbles/shingle: Golden sand along a narrow strip beach extends to and beyond the waterline.
Sunbeds/umbrellas: No.
Showers: No.
Safe for children: This is a placid seascape. The water is shallow and it's good for youngsters.
Watersports: No.
Main users: Locals.

eSCAPE tO tHE... beaches

Well cared for: Comparatively.
Mooring for boats: No.
Next to quayside/harbour: No.
Storm drains/outlets into sea: Storm drains.
Natural shady areas: No. The beach is largely exposed although there is a little shade from the cliffs behind.

beaches

Any other facilities: Rooms to let.
Distance to main resorts: Zakynthos is about 15 km.
Public transport: Buses pass relatively close by, although you'll have to walk the last of the route. Alternately, utilise independent transport or telephone for a taxi.
Blue Flag: No.

Shoestring (Old Alykanas)
Σαγιονάρα (Παλιός Αλικανάς)

$$\frac{155}{250}$$ ★★★★

Beach location: Follow the beach signs from the T Junction in Alykanas.
Then, when you reach the signpost for Ag. Kiriaki, turn right rather than left

and keep going until you come across the unofficial beach signs on the Shoestring Taverna.

Disabled access: No. There are steep paths and steps to this beach.

Car parking: Parking is only available on the roadside. It's narrow but normally possible to park.

Food outlets/restaurants: Yes. There are two or three facilities located behind the beach.

Sand/pebbles/shingle: Soft golden sand.

153

Sunbeds/umbrellas: Yes.

Showers: No.

Safe for children: The sea here is relatively gentle but there can be some waves and it shelves deeply in places. There are tidal sand spits and some large submerged rocks to contend with.

Watersports: No.

Main users: Tourists and locals.

Well cared for: The sea can be a little murky although the water is not dirty. Spoiled a little by litter.

Mooring for boats: Small craft can tie up at the breakwaters. Larger craft can moor off.

Next to quayside/harbour: No.

Storm drains/outlets into sea: No.

Natural shady areas: There are grassy cliffs behind he beach but these provide little shade.

Any other facilities: Rooms to let and a mini-market close by.

Distance to main resorts: 4 km. from Alykanas.
Public transport: No.
Blue Flag: No.

Smugglers Wreck (Navagio)
Ναυάγιο

$$\frac{80}{250}$$

Beach location: You will see this beach on every tourist brochure featuring Zakynthos. In reality it's best viewed from a distance and not really worth a visit except out of curiosity. You have to reach it by boat - either an organised trip around the island or a water taxi from Porto Vromi or one of the other northern harbours. Come for an hour - not for a day trip.

Disabled access: You must be able to drop from a boat and climb back onboard.

Car parking: Don't be silly!

Food outlets/restaurants: No - absolutely nothing.

Sand/pebbles/shingle: Fine shingle and small pebbles face an amazing electric blue sea.

Sunbeds/umbrellas: No.

Showers: No.

Safe for children: Relatively. However, the water goes deep quickly and there is some oil. The rusting hulk of the Panagiotis is a magnet for youngsters but not the safest thing to be clambering all over.

Watersports: No.

Main users: Tourists.

Well cared for: No. Oil, scrap metal and glass coupled with stinging weeds in places. No litter bins and no facilities.

Mooring for boats: Trip boats monopolise the shoreline. However, you can moor off in the bay with little difficulty.

Next to quayside/harbour: No. However, the constant procession of trip boats leaves its mark on the local environment.

Storm drains/outlets into sea: No.

Natural shady areas: No.

Any other facilities: No.

Distance to main resorts: Zakynthos is between thirty and forty kilometres distant - not that you can get to the beach by road anyway.

Public transport: No.

Blue Flag: No.

eSCAPE tO tHE... beaches

Spianza (Banana Beach)
Σπάντζα (Μπανάνα)

$$\frac{165}{250}$$

Beach location: From the main Vassilikos Road, you follow an unmade track situated about 1km. before the turning for St. Nicholas Beach. Turn left (it tends to be signposted as Banana rather than Spianza) and proceed

through the sand dunes. The track will drop you into a parking area.
Disabled access: It's just about possible but wheelchairs will struggle.
Car parking: Yes. However, it gets very busy in high season and can be full.
Food outlets/restaurants: There are three or four beach bars spread out along the beach.
Sand/pebbles/shingle: Golden sand, with some small pebbles beyond the waterline.
Sunbeds/umbrellas: Yes.

Showers: Yes and maybe a toilet associated with one or two of the beach bars. It depends where you park and patronise.

Safe for children: Relatively. However, bear in mind this is open sea. It gets very windy and there are strong tides and currents running.

Watersports: No.

Main users: Mainly locals, plus a few tourists who've found it.

Well cared for: Yes.

Mooring for boats: No.

Next to quayside/harbour: No.
Storm drains/outlets into sea: No.
Natural shady areas: This is an exposed beach and gets quite windswept. There is no natural shade.
Any other facilities: A few rooms to let close by.
Distance to main resorts: Argassi 10 km. Zakynthos 15 km.
Public transport: No. Independent transport required.
Blue Flag: No.

eSCAPE to THE... beaches

eSCAPE eSCAPE to THE... beaches

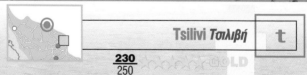

Tsilivi *Τσιλιβή*

t

230
250

GOLD

Beach location: Signposted from the resort, with access at a number of points along the coastal road. There are also nearby beaches at Planos and Bouka. Depending on where your accommodation is located, you will be between .25 km. and 1 km. of the beach

beaches

Disabled access: Yes.
Car parking: Yes. However, parking at the beach itself is somewhat limited. If full, park on the road where possible and walk.
Food outlets/restaurants: Yes. Dozens and dozens!
Sand/pebbles/shingle: Deep golden sand sweeps over a wide area.
Sunbeds/umbrellas: Yes.
Showers: Yes.
Safe for children: The water is placid and shallow, even though it faces out to the open sea, making it relatively safe for children.

eSCAPE

beaches

Watersports: Yes.
Main users: Tourists.
Well cared for: Yes.
Mooring for boats: No.
Next to quayside/harbour: No.
Storm drains/outlets into sea: None observed.

Natural shady areas: The beach is very exposed.
Any other facilities: Full resort facilities.
Distance to main resorts: 0 - 1 km. depending on the location of your accommodation.
Public transport: Buses and taxis serve the resort.
Blue Flag: Yes.

ionian
ato**z**

I am old and poor.
I ask for some tips
to keep myself alive
in my elderness. I can
offer walks and photos

O Vasilis   1.50€

Accommodation

Accommodation is routinely available throughout the Ionian and varies from luxury hotels to the most basic of self catering accommodation and «rooms». Price is often a fair reflection of facilities and, if it sounds too cheap, it probably is! Hotels are graded luxury and then A to E with E representing the lowest standard. Rooms tend to be graded A to C but there is much more of a blur around their standard. Some rooms consist of little more than a sparsely furnished spare bedroom. Others are well appointed in purpose built blocks with bars, swimming pools and sometimes restaurant facilities.

You do not need to pre-book accommodation except, perhaps, in August. Otherwise, you can just turn up, inspect the accommodation and, if satisfied, conclude a deal over the price per night. This is often the cheapest way but you must be prepared to haggle. Check the door certificate which must be displayed by law. That gives you indicative prices. Never pay more; preferably seek to pay considerably less.

Internet agencies such as www.islandsofdreams.com may throw up cheap options and you can also consult the local tourist board or Tourist Police. Many commercial agencies will offer local accommodation, along with safety deposit facilities and even cooling fans and alarm clocks! Always ask to view the accommodation first and don't accept it if you are not 100% happy with what you see. If it doesn't look good when you are first shown it, it certainly won't look any better by the end of your first night! If you're really stuck, book for one night and review the possibilities the next morning.

Airports

With the single exception of Eleftherios Venizelos Airport in Athens, most Greek airports leave much to be desired. The Ionian is no exception, with a combination of ageing military and somewhat inadequate, albeit more modern, civil airports serving the interests of its travelling public. Corfu, Cephalonia and Zakynthos possess their own airports. Lefkas and Parga are served by a combined military and civil facility at mainland Preveza (Aktion) - some distance away from both resort areas. The facilities on Corfu and Zakynthos are relatively central to the resorts.

Cephalonia's airport, however, is to the south of the island but close to Argostoli (for Lassi and Skala).

Irrespective of whether the airport is civil or military, photography inside or nearby is forbidden. As with most airports, prices charged in the inadequate cafes are outrageous. Terminals are inevitably too small for planes that now disgorge up to 200 passengers per flight. Equally, the recent tendency of package tour companies to bring a number of flights in at broadly the same time exacerbates the problems further. Departing passengers are particularly badly hit and tend to wait in hot, claustrophobic, overcrowded conditions with little to do other than spend their few remaining Euro on the tired looking, limited tourist offerings available to purchase. There are often long queues at the departure check-in. It is advisable to get there early, check and recheck that you are in the correct queue and not to trust blindly the information on monitors or other notices displayed around the departure hall.

Passports or other photographic evidence of identity is now required even for domestic flights. All hold baggage is x-rayed and cabin luggage may additionally be hand searched. No sharp implements may be carried onto a flight. Offending items such as nail-files, scissors or penknives will be confiscated.

Stowed baggage allowances for international flights are normally 20 kilos. For domestic flights, you are allowed 15 kilos. However, overweight bags are seldom a problem. Cabin baggage can be more problematic and the 5 kilo rule is often enforced (but remember it's plus a laptop, camera, purse or wallet). Ionian airports tend not to have sufficient baggage trolleys and you may have to pay (with a 1 or 2 euro coin) to utilise one. Most airports have a «Duty Paid» shop and these can offer genuine bargains in home produced liquor such as ouzo and brandy, along with olives, cheese, nuts and tobacco products. It will still almost certainly be possible to find the same products cheaper in your resort and airport shopping is best saved for that last-minute impulse buy.

Taxis tend to stand in ranks outside most airports and, otherwise, are summoned via courtesy phones dotted around the terminal. There are extra charges for airport journeys, the number of bags carried and travel after midnight. Always agree a price with your taxi driver before you commence the journey. This is particularly important on arrival if you are unfamiliar with the currency and distance involved. Most taxi drivers are honest but some are not. If the journey doesn't seem cheaper than you would expect to pay at home, beware!

Ambulance - phone **166**

Banks

Banks can normally be found in the main towns of each Ionian island. Lately, some have opened branches in tourist resorts, although this is by no means universal. Most have cash dispensers (Automated Teller Machines) and some have currency exchange machines which accept foreign notes and convert them to euro bills - at a price. Another recent development is an ATM "cluster" prominently located in some of the major resorts. As long as you have a Visa or Mastercard (and occasionally American Express) credit card (or certain debit cards) with a pin number, you will be able to withdraw funds from these machines. Services are available in different languages - most usually Greek and English. Banks also exchange travellers' cheques and normally the rate offered is higher but subject to a commission fee. Hotels tend not to charge commission but may offer a lower exchange rate. Shop around. You will need your passport to exchange travellers' cheques.

On balance, using a suitable debit card is probably both the cheapest and safest option. You will need to check with your bank that your card is suitable for use abroad before departure.

Banking hours are normally 8 or 8.30 a.m. to 2 p.m. from Monday to Thursday. On Friday they close at 1 or 1.30 p.m. They do not re-open after the afternoon siesta time and remain closed at weekends. There may be local variances in the opening hours. It is advisable not to rely on the fact there will be an ATM machine in your resort. Carrying some travellers' cheques is both advisable and more secure than carrying cash. Do not keep all your funds in one place and, preferably, make use of safe deposit facilities at hotels and major self-catering facilities.

Bomba

This is the local term given to commercial alcohol which is sometimes added by unscrupulous bar owners to drinks instead of proprietary brands of spirits. Most often, those who drink cocktails - where the spirit is well masked by fruit juices or cream - are the sufferers. However, mixed drinks containing vodka can also sometimes be doctored. While the results are seldom fatal, you can get the most awful reaction which feels like a massive hangover coupled with the flu. Best advice is to drink spirits only in bars you are 100% confident about - such as major hotel cocktail bars or those recommended by locals.

Buses

With the exception of Corfu, which has an additional local bus service (and tiny Meganissi which has its own municipal mini-bus!), Ionian Islands are served by KTEL Buses (the national operator). Normally recognisable from their dingy petrol blue-green and cream livery, a fleet of single-deck coaches traverses the major Ionian islands. Services can be helpful in getting you around an island but are also invaluable for those who want to hop between islands or visit major mainland cities. The advent of internet cafes in the Ionian means that it is now possible to access the KTEL website locally, thereby discovering all the services that are routinely available on the island of your choice. Go to www.ktel.org for information (currently Zakynthos is not featured on the site).

Regular services exist to most resorts. Occasional services to more remote, interior villages cater principally for local residents and school students. There are express routes to Greece's third largest city, Patras and to the Capital, Athens - useful in both cases as this provides a cheap and cheerful way of reaching major ferry ports. Timetables frequently change and advance booking on the express routes is strongly advisable.

It is not unknown (though infrequent these days) to share your local journey with a chicken or goat and the express routes provide six to ten hours of bottom-numbing boredom in hot, crowded and a sometimes less than delicately scented environment!

Car Rental

Car and motorbike rental is widely available throughout the Ionian. International companies are well represented with local franchises in most of the main towns and local companies are found in many of the resorts. An alternative is to pre-book via your travel agent or on the internet - often at cheaper rates than are routinely available in Greece itself.

In addition to needing to «haggle» for the best price, it is imperative that you check carefully that you are being afforded full insurance. Many Greek companies have incomprehensible agreements versed in pigeon English. If it comes to an argument, you are in their country and unlikely to come out on top.

Seek fully comprehensive insurance with the smallest damage penalties or excess possible. If damage is going to cost you more than 500 Euro, the insurance policy is doubtful.

Motor bikes must be hired with crash helmets and these must be worn by law. Although this is cursed by the "macho" Greeks, police now regularly enforce their wearing and spot fines will be awarded against offenders.

Chemists See pharmacies

Contraception

Sheaths are routinely available from supermarkets and chemists. Rather interesting titles such as «Rabbit», «Stop» and «No Aids» seem to sell well to tourists! Female contraception is more problematic and it is advisable to bring your own from the UK. Most pharmacies stock the contraceptive pill. In case of difficulties consult a local doctor.

Credit Cards

The use of credit (and latterly debit) cards has extended significantly over the last decade and they are now welcomed at many establishments throughout the Ionian. Authorisation procedures have also improved and most establishments now have their own instantaneous, electronic facility. Most merchants will accept either Mastercard or, more commonly, Visa. A strictly limited number of establishments accept American Express or Diners Card. If you are "haggling" for a bargain in such as a jeweller's store, don't be surprised if you are offered different discounts according to the card you proffer. Commission rates charged to merchants vary from company to company and this will be reflected in the discount you are offered.

If your card becomes unusable during your Ionian trip, this may be because the credit card company suspects that it is being inappropriately used in unfamiliar surroundings. A phone call to your card provider will rapidly resolve matters. Equally, when using an ATM, service is sometimes suspended when your request gets mangled in cyberspace. Don't try more than twice at any one time or the machine is likely to retain your card! Leave it twenty-four hours and then try again - or use a different machine or card, if possible.

Currency

The Greek currency is now the Euro. One Euro is currently slightly more than an American dollar. £1 sterling will currently buy approximately 1.40 euro. Notes exist in denominations as large as 500 Euro but you will be less than welcome anywhere if you offer anything above 50! The most normal notes are 50, 20, 10 and 5 with coins of 2 and 1 euro. Small change (50, 20, 10, 5, 2 and 1 cent coins) will soon weigh down your pocket - especially while you remain unfamiliar with the value of the currency.

In the last ten years, Greece has relaxed its currency importation regulations although you will routinely see currency declaration notices at airports. Unless you are bringing extremely large sums in or out of the country, this should not concern you. However, if you are planning a major cash transaction it is sensible to seek advice from the Greek Embassy in your own country or, preferably, your own embassy if you are already in Greece.

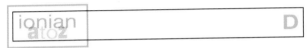

Dentists

Dental facilities are relatively scarce in the Ionian and inevitably centred on the main town on each of the islands. The local tourist information office will probably be able to assist with the location of nearby facilities. (If the assistant here greets you with a beaming gold and mercury laden smile, you may find it sensible to decline their advice as to the best local dentist!). Get a receipt from the dentist if you intend to make a travel insurance claim.

Diarrhoea

A change in water supply, too much alcohol or an olive that's past its sell-by date - all can set off the dreaded "runs". It is best to bring a packet of your favourite remedy (such as Arret or Imodium) with you from the UK. There are also local versions, available from pharmacies. Recovery will be best assisted if you eat little and drink plenty of non-alcoholic fluids. If diarrhoea persists for more than a couple of days, consult a doctor.

Disabled Access

Many disabled people visit the Ionian but how they manage is a matter of amazement. Wheelchair users and the visually impaired will find frequently changing pavement levels in many town centre streets a problem. Shop displays spill out onto the side-walk, forcing even the ambulant to risk injury by venturing out into the road. In the resorts, roads seldom have areas reserved for pedestrians and there are often ditches at the roadside to contend with as well. It is almost routine to find a car parked across road junctions at the point pedestrians are expected to cross. Unexpected holes, seemingly abandoned road-works and scaffolding that completely blocks pedestrian thoroughfares are all too frequent.

In the vast majority of cases, tavernas and bars have narrow toilets - often located up or down steps or in relatively inaccessible corners. These are a nightmare for wheelchair users. It is also important to check the suitability of your accommodation in advance. Larger hotels will have lifts but may be approached up steep, ornate, external steps. Alternately, the lift may have no internal door or be too narrow for a wheelchair. Some accommodation may be high in the hillside, a fierce climb even for the fit! Check before you book. Self-catering accommodation will only be accessible at ground floor level - if that.

Finally beaches, often including those that have somehow managed to acquire a European Blue Flag, have less than impressive disabled access points (if any) and disabled toilets are virtually unknown.

Things are beginning to change but it is a slow and tedious transition. In the meantime, wheelchair users and the visually impaired, in particular, would be advised to check carefully regarding access before embarking on any particular excursion.

Diving

It is possible to hire equipment and to obtain tuition on most of the Ionian Islands. Check with your tour company representative or hotel receptionist. There are often fly-posted signs advertising diving facilities in the resorts. You must satisfy yourself that the standard of tuition in any diving school you consider using is appropriate and that the person training you is qualified to provide tuition. It's also imperative to check your travel insurance before engaging in this activity as you may not be covered if something goes wrong.

Doctors

All Ionian Islands have at least one (and frequently several) local doctors. Recently, medical facilities in resorts have started to increase significantly and only the smaller local resorts are now unlikely to have their own practitioner. Sometimes, even if there is no doctor, the resort may have a pharmacy and staff there will probably be able to assist.

Hotels and tour companies tend to have arrangements with local doctors to undertake house calls. Expect to pay for the consultation there and then in local currency. Obtain a receipt for any claim against travel insurance.

In Greece, doctors tend to specialise so, for instance, if mosquitoes are troublesome you should seek the assistance of the local dermatologist. In more serious cases, you may even find yourself being referred from smaller hospitals to these specialist local consultants.

Duty Free Goods

Alas, the days of duty free sales (within the EU) have gone and only those entering from outside of the EU and returning to a destination outside of the EU are entitled to import and export duty free goods.

Duty paid goods are often a good bargain and tobacco (in all its forms) is significantly cheaper than the UK. The same is true of wines and spirits as well as local produce such as pistachio nuts, cheese, olives and olive oil. Theoretically, those purchasing goods in Greece for personal use elsewhere within the EU can carry as much as they want. You may find yourself having to prove that the goods are for your personal use on arrival at your home destination. More immediately, you may also find that your airline will either not carry overweight cases or, alternately, extracts a significant sum per kilo from you for the privilege. This can nullify the bargain price you've paid!

ionian a to z   E

Earth Tremors

Many populated areas of the Ionian were almost completely destroyed in 1953 by a huge earthquake. Mild earth tremors are a frequent reminder of the volatility of the surroundings. All buildings are now constructed to withstand shocks and a reasonably strong tremor will shake you no more than a journey in a lift. Building regulations also limit the height of all constructions to enhance safety.

Electricity Supply

Electricity supply is 220 volts a.c. Sockets are of the round two pin variety and you can purchase adaptors reasonably easily at airports, travel shops or in your resort supermarket.

EMERGENCY PHONE NUMBERS		
AMBULANCE: **166**		
ENGLISH LANGUAGE EMERGENCY CALL NUMBER: **112**		
FIRE: **199**	POLICE: **100**	TOURIST POLICE: **171**

IONIAN
a to z

f

ionian
a to z

USEFUL iNFORMATION

USEFUL iNFORMATION

F

Ferries

The Ionian Islands are quite well connected by ferry services and it is possible to travel up and down the chain, as well as making connections with various mainland ports of call. A limited international service runs between Italy, certain of the islands and Patras on the mainland. Many ferry services operate at least daily. Most operate several times per day.

> Patras is the hub for major Ionian services. From here, you can reach Cephalonia, Ithaca, Corfu and (occasionally) Paxos. You can also reach Igoumentisa on the mainland (and from there Corfu or Paxos). In certain cases, you will need a domestic ticket on an international service whose ultimate stop will be one of the Italian ports. For some obscure reason, domestic tickets are not well advertised and, indeed, some lines will not take domestic leg passengers. You need to check locally.

From Cephalonia, there are local services to Ithaca, Lefkas and Zakynthos. There are also services to the mainland and you can explore the delights of Killini (not recommended except as a stop-over to get to Zakynthos) or Astakos (marginally more interesting but not as exciting as watching paint dry). Most services feature landing craft style ferries and are quite slow. There is also a very useful cross-bay service between Argostoli and Lixouri (Cephalonia's two largest towns) and this saves you many miles of hard driving otherwise. One thing to beware of - there is no "main" port for Cephalonia (although Sami is tending to adopt this role). Thus you will have to check carefully the port of departure for your desired service as they have a habit of changing!

From Corfu, there are local services to mainland Igoumenitsa from Corfu Town and the small harbour at Lefkimmi in the south of the island. You can also take a ferry to Paxos (although sometimes it's quicker to take one of the many trip boats offering this journey). Landing craft ferries take best part of two hours to cross from the mainland to Corfu. The larger roll-on, roll-off ferries do the trip in about an hour. Catamaran and hydrofoil services come and go but are passenger only. The tiny Diaspondia Islands, Parga and even Albania can be visited from Corfu with services operating from the port at Corfu Town and some of the northern resorts.

Ithaca is a satellite of Cephalonia but does not feature heavily in the tourism stakes. Ferries from Patras normally travel on from Cephalonia to Ithaca before turning round for the reverse trip. There are also services from Sami and Fiskardo, as well as a significant number of trip boats that make the excursion. The Fiskardo service travels beyond Ithaca, extending as far as Lefkas.

From Lefkas, you can travel south to both Cephalonia and Ithaca. There are also trip boats offering the mainland resort of Parga as well as the island of Paxos. Lefkas Town is joined to the mainland by a causeway and it's perfectly possible to visit Parga with a hire car in one day. You can also take this coastal route further north in order to visit Paxos or Corfu but would be wiser to include an overnight stop in such an itinerary.

Meganissi - despite meaning big island - is actually so small as not to be classed as an Ionian Island. Yet it is a beautiful place to visit and can be reached in little over half an hour from Nidri on Lefkas. There are several departures daily and trip boats also frequently offer this excursion. Services linking Meganissi with other islands have come and gone. For the time being, the journey from Nidri represents the safest bet.

From Zakynthos there is but one island you can visit - Cephalonia. A ferry route runs from northern Zakynthos to southern Cephalonia on a daily basis. Otherwise, the "charms" of mainland Killini await you, as this is the only other ferry route operational. From Killini, you can also reach Cephalonia by ferry and it is a short distance by road (or bus) to Patras, the main Ionian ferry hub. Hydrofoil services linking Zakynthos with other Ionian islands have come and gone and currently seem unlikely to return.

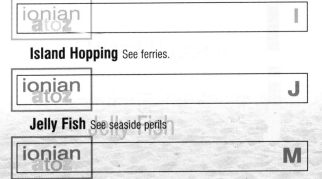

ionian
ato2   I

Island Hopping See ferries.

ionian
ato2   J

Jelly Fish See seaside perils

ionian
ato   M

Maps
Maps are available from tourist shops and kiosks. Their descriptions

should be treated with scepticism. Some maps show roads that simply do not exist and sometimes you will find locations spelled differently or, more problematically, appearing at a different point on the map than that encountered on your journey!

Beware of sudden deterioration in road conditions not evident from the map. This is not indicative that your road is necessarily about to give out, however it does suggest that you proceed only with great caution and at an appropriate speed. Secondary roads can go from tarmac to dirt track within a few metres! Go for the most recently published editions and preferably buy two different maps. You may have some hope of reaching your destination by comparing one with the other as you travel along!

Medical Insurance

In theory, every EU citizen is entitled to free hospital treatment wherever they travel in Europe. Indeed, there is a special form (E111) that is supposed to travel with you, wherever you go, in anticipation of a claim. However, in Greece it is (a) seldom demanded and (b) gets you only the lowest grade of state hospital attention. It is therefore strongly advisable to purchase medical insurance before departure and to have your copy of the policy - and the access number to initiate a claim - close to hand, throughout your holiday.

Mosquitoes

Mosquitoes can be troublesome throughout the season particularly in damp areas or near foliage. Many preparations are available to apply to exposed skin both from the UK and in local pharmacies and supermarkets. It is advisable to get a plug in machine for your bedroom and to keep windows closed at night. There are three types of machines available locally. The first version is a slow-burning coil of a pretty obnoxious chemical preparation disguised with an incense aroma. In the second version you heat a fresh tablet (supplied separately in packets of 10 to 30 tablets) each night to provide a mosquito free environment. These tend to be quite effective but again the main ingredient is a strong chemical that may not suit your metabolism. The third version is a variation on the second - except it has its own reservoir of liquid chemical that is infused and vaporised. This saves buying the separate tablets.

One or two bites are simply unpleasant but, with greater numbers, an allergic reaction can set in. Eruptions the size of grapes can break out and there is great discomfort. If you suffer from such a reaction try and locate a dermatologist who will be able to treat this condition. As a general precaution if bitten avoid fish, eggs and pork and cover all exposed skin.

Naturism

Strictly speaking, naturism on public beaches is illegal. However, it is tolerated on certain beaches - normally at the «extremities». Take local advice before you indulge. Over-zealous members of the police force are known to relish occasional purges. Arrest and a fine can ensue.

Newspapers

Newspapers from the UK and other European countries routinely reach the Ionian the day after publication. A premium price for their air flight is charged with a tabloid edition costing between 1 and 2 euro. A more recent development, thanks to the wonders of technology has resulted in European editions being printed more locally, which means you can now sometimes get your favourite read the same day.

As an alternative, the International Herald Tribune contains an insert with an English language translation of the Greek daily «Kathimerini». Not only do you get a local slant on national and international affairs, it's also extremely helpful in pre-warning you about impending strikes that might be about to close airports, ferry terminals or petrol stations! The advent of this daily has also seen the demise of the excellent Athens News, which was published in English each day, but now surfaces only weekly. It's published each Friday and tends to be available at limited news agencies and kiosks on each island.

It also has a free website at **www.athensnews.gr**

Opening Hours

Shops in the main towns tend to open from about 8 a.m. until 2 p.m. and then close for an eminently sensible siesta until about 5.30 p.m. On about three days per week, they then spring back to life, remaining open until 8 p.m. or later.

In the resorts, it's a different story with most establishments remaining open all day and late into the evening, seven days a week, throughout the season.

Petrol Station

Normal opening hours are 7 a.m. to 7 p.m. with summer extensions to 8 p.m. Weekend opening (particularly Sunday), public holidays and saints' days can all bring restrictions or closures. Prices are cheaper than the U.K. and more expensive than the U.S.A. Most hire cars take unleaded petrol. Diesel tends to be known as Gaz-Oil. Small motorbikes may use a two-stroke mixture of petrol and oil - you need to check! There are very few self-service facilities and the attendant who serves you will invariably get the type of fuel right, even if you're not quite sure! It's advisable not to trust that there will always be a filling station on your route. So don't let your tank go under half full without filling up.

A welcome recent development has been the opening of car wash facilities at some of the larger filling stations. If you are travelling any distance, you will be surprised just how dusty the car gets in a relatively short time.

Pharmacies

There are pharmacies on all the Ionian Islands. Normally located in the main town, you will also discover them in a number of the resorts. Recognisable by the red or green cross outside or in the window, the Greek word is similar to the English for pharmacy, «FARMAKIO».

English is normally well spoken (other European languages, less so) and opening hours are generally the same or a little longer than the local shops. However, there is also an out-of-hours emergency duty rota and this is displayed in the windows of those shops which are closed (unfortunately, often only in Greek).

A wide range of remedies is available without prescription. You can also consult a pharmacist for a potential remedy for minor ailments and this can save you the time and expense of a doctor's consultation. Keep pharmacy receipts for any insurance claim.

Police

There are three distinct «**arms**» of the law in Greece.

There are civil police stations in main towns, a number of the larger villages and resorts throughout the Ionian. Language can be a barrier and, for this reason, you may wish to make use of the Tourist Police Service. Tourist Police Officers are a cross between a normal police officer and a trading standards officer. They are there to ensure that regulations governing the operation of tourist facilities are observed and are relatively fluent in at least one foreign language (normally English).

While Tourist Police Officers are not there as your «advocate», they can be helpful in defusing disputes between traders or hoteliers and their tourist clients. Do not lose sight of the fact, however, that they have all the powers of the normal police force and can just as easily arrest tourists whose behaviour they believe to be unreasonable.

The third strand of the Police Service is the nattily clad Port Police, whose all - white marine uniform has sent many a female heart (and some male ones!) fluttering. Responsible for conduct of ferry arrivals and departures, you will probably hear one before you see one. Armed with the statutory whistle, which is blown continuously, their job is to ensure that passengers and vehicles embark and disembark safely and sensibly. Normally equipped with good English, they are a fairly reliable source of information on ferry movements.

EMERGENCY POLICE TELEPHONE NUMBER: **100**
TOURIST POLICE NUMBER: **171**
ENGLISH LANGUAGE EMERGENCY CALL NUMBER: **112**

Postal Facilities

Those wanting to send postcards and expecting them to arrive home before they do would be advised to send them early in their holiday from a main post office. There are plenty of yellow post boxes nailed to trees or lamp posts in the various resorts but collections are spasmodic. Stamps for your cards will often be sold with them - ask when you purchase. Hotels are always helpful in providing stamps and will often post your cards for you as well. Most post offices are open from Monday to Friday between 7.30 a.m. and 1 p.m. Some post offices have extended opening hours. Main post offices are located in principal towns but there are also outlets in a number of resorts and some inland villages.

ionian a to z   **R**

Rainfall

It is difficult to be prescriptive about rainfall albeit that this is of vital interest to most tourists. Rainfall may consist of nothing more than a few spots or, alternately, a savage thunderstorm in which streets become rivers and you have to wade across the road! As a broad indication, the average number of days on which you can expect (some) rain to fall on a monthly basis are as follows:

•	January	- 14	• July	- 1
•	February	- 13	• August	- 2
•	March	- 11	• September	- 5
•	April	- 8	• October	- 11
•	May	- 6	• November	- 14
•	June	- 4	• December	- 18

Restaurants

When referring to restaurants, the Greeks differentiate between the «Taverna» and the «Estiatorio» - the latter purportedly equating more to a high-class restaurant. In the Ionian, the situation is much more blurred. There are some restaurants with fancy tablecloths and little more to recommend them and ones with paper tablecloths and wonderful, freshly prepared, mouth-watering dishes.

Prices are no longer the «cheap treat» that they used to be although you can still find good bargains if you hunt around. Best bet is to avoid the tourist haunts and seek out where the locals go. Here the food will be good and the prices more reasonable. Credit cards are now almost universally accepted in the more up-market restaurants. However, you may find cash only is accepted in more local establishments.

House wine is likely to be home produced and served by the kilo from a large barrel but it's cheap and cheerful (rocket fuel basically!) and not too bad tasting. Unless you like the taste of disinfectant, you may wish to give the pine-resin impregnated flavour of the local wine "Retsina" a miss. While "barrel" wine is very cheap, you may still prefer to taste it before buying a whole kilo! If it's not to your taste, ask for a bottle of a proprietary brand like Tsantali, Robola or Boutari instead.

In addition to Greek specialities, the influence of the Venetians is still retained throughout the Ionian and there are many restaurants serving excellent Italian food. You will also find a sprinkling of Indian, Chinese and Tex-Mex establishments. Occasionally, you will come across even more unusual offerings-Thai food and even the odd Russian Restaurant! Vegetarian restaurants are few and far between however, you will find vegetarian offerings routinely included on most menus (particularly among the starters).

Fish restaurants abound, as you might expect in the Ionian. The prices here tend to be more expensive than you would routinely like to pay. Fish is normally offered on menus by the kilo - so the price isn't quite as bad as it looks. As you are unlikely to eat this much, ask for advice on a suit-able amount per person. Your waiter should be more than happy to show you what's available in the kitchen and, with some helpful advice, let you choose how much you'd like.

Greece has happily adopted the «burger bar» and you may even find the odd McDonald's! Otherwise, there are plenty of local variants offering a similar staple diet. The traditional Greek fast-food eatery dispenses «sou-vlaki pita» (small cuts of meat, normally pork, in a warm spongy, waffle-like «bun»). This is the equivalent of the English fish and chip shop - albeit the products on offer are different - and you will also find a number of other tasty (meat) dishes including Kontosouvli and the more familiar breast of chicken. Chips are also available in plentiful supply. These places are cheap and cheerful with eat-in and take-away facilities routinely available.

Room Rates

Each hotel or self-catering establishment is required by law to dis-play the charge for the room on a certificate which can normally be found on the back of the door. The rate is per room and not per person. Package tourists can see what they would have paid, had they made their own arrangements! These are maximum prices and discounts can be nego-ti-ated. Air conditioning, a fridge in the room, breakfast etc., is sometimes charged extra. The rates can also vary at high and low season. See also the section on accommodation.

ionian
atoz   S

Safety Deposit Boxes

Whilst the integrity and honesty of the islanders is without question, the same cannot necessarily be said of other tourists or the influx of ille-gal immigrants from places like Albania, Bulgaria and Romania. It is advis-able therefore to acquire a safety deposit box at a hotel or self-catering complex. Facilities may also be offered to non- residents. Costs are very small per week.

Scorpions See seaside perils.

Seaside Perils

There are two frequent offenders. Firstly, sea urchins will be found on most rocky coastlines in the Ionian. These small spiky «balls» frequently end up embedding a spine or two into the tender feet of unsuspecting tourists. Prevention is the best cure so wear suitable footwear when swimming or exploring around rocky areas. If you do get a spine embedded, don't pull it straight out as it will rip the skin and spread the poison. It's best to break or cut the spine close to the foot, then apply olive oil to soften the area around the spine. Remove it later, when it feels softer and easier and disinfect the area well. Do not ignore a spine as it will simply get worse.

From time to time, the tides also bring in jellyfish and these can vary in size and intensity of sting. You can get local remedies in pharmacies. Otherwise it's grin and bear it for up to 24 hours, by which time the worst effects should have diminished.

Very occasionally, you may encounter a small scorpion on the beach. These are not particularly poisonous and they certainly do not possess a fatal sting. There are also one or two local fish that possess venomous spines. The good news is that they're extremely rare. The bad news is that they can inflict permanent damage! So if you are stung by a fish (and the pain is intense - so you will know) seek immediate local help.

Sea Urchins See seaside perils.

Sizes

If you're thinking of purchasing clothes or footwear (which is often a bargain) you may find the following conversion chart of assistance:

women's clothes (dress/bust sizes)					
UK	10/32	12/34	14/36	16/38	18/40
Greece	42	44	46	48	50
men's clothes (chest sizes)						
UK	36	38	40	42	44	46
Greece	46	48	50	52	54	56
shirt (neck) sizes					
UK	14	15	16	17	18
Greece	37	38	40	42	43
shoe sizes								
UK	3	4	5	6	7	8	9	10	11
Greece	36	37	38	39	40	41	42	43	44

Snakes

The further into the countryside your accommodation, the more likely you are to encounter a snake. The average snake wants to get out of your way a lot more than you want to get away from it. Nevertheless, it can give you something of a shock if you pick up a rock to discover one underneath, having a snooze! There's marginally more danger if you tread on one inadvertently during a countryside walk. Snakes can exceed one metre in length and look fierce, even though they're harmless. They can also be pencil slim and a matter of inches long and you'll quite often see this sort wriggling across the road in more remote locations. The best bet is to stick to open paths and wear footwear which covers your feet and ankles when crossing rough country. There are only one or two varieties of snakes that are venomous (adders basically). With prompt treatment, their bite is not fatal and they go nowhere near tourist areas. There are also small, virtually colourless, scorpions. If bitten, seek immediate medical attention.

ionian a to z   **T**

Taxis

Taxis ply for hire across all the islands. Corfu has several hundred, tiny Meganissi has but one! They are inexpensive and relatively comfortable. At times of high demand, you are best to phone for a taxi as there can be a shortage available to «flag» on the road (or they may ignore you). Most taxi drivers are honest but it is known for them to deliberately overcharge - especially on your first trip from the airport. They also have «interesting» driving techniques including arm waving, horn pounding and resorting to frank vocalizations of their opinions of other road users parentage! It appears mandatory for them to possess and seek to utilize at least one mobile phone whilst driving.

There are some «rules» you need to know. Journeys to airports and bus stations cost extra (don't ask why!), excess luggage is chargeable and it costs more after midnight. When you phone a cab, you pay from the point of its departure - not where it picks you up. It is also legal to share a taxi in Greece (indeed in Athens you probably won't get one unless you share it). In such instances, you will still pay full fare as will the other customer(s) who may be going to exactly the same place. A good hint at busy taxi ranks is to see whether other tourists are going to the same place you are. In this way, if you all purport to be travelling together, you can split the fare between you - rather than pay full fare twice over.

Telephones

The telephone system has been much improved in the last decade. Gone is the need to travel to the local telephone exchange in order to place an international call. The cheapest method is now from the many OTE card-phone booths dotted all over the islands (even at remote beaches) with phone cards readily available from supermarkets and kiosks.

Phone calls from hotels and supermarkets are metered. You will pay a surcharge. The number of units showing on the meter does not necessarily reflect the cost of your call - it may be significantly more. Check first! At the telephone exchange, where you can still make international calls, the amount of the call is normally the figure showing on the meter.

Greece has discovered the mobile phone! Indeed it's one of the biggest users in Europe! You can normally arrange with your own service provider to allow «roaming» on the Greek system, allowing you to take your mobile with you. Beware the charges for this facility - they're very expensive. You will also find that you're paying the international element of costs associated with calls made to your mobile from other countries as well as your own outgoing calls.

The international code for Greece is 00 30

Temperature

The seasonal temperature varies from island to island and, indeed, can vary by five or ten degrees between resorts on a day to day basis. A broad average is given below (in Fahrenheit). Actual maximum temperatures frequently exceed those shown. After noon until late afternoon, the temperature can routinely exceed 90 degrees Fahrenheit in the height of summer.

Month	-	°F	Month	-	°F
January	-	52	July	-	80
February	-	50	August	-	80
March	-	54	September	-	76
April	-	58	October	-	68
May	-	66	November	-	62
June	-	74	December	-	56

Time Zone

Greece is two hours ahead of the UK and one hour ahead of most of the remainder of Europe. Daylight saving is followed and clocks are switched forward and back by one hour - normally in April and late October - as per the rest of Europe.

Tipping

Tipping is acceptable, although the 10 - 15 % associated with Europe and the USA will seldom be expected. A cover charge added to the cost of your meal represents only the cost of the basket of bread placed on your table almost as soon as you sit down and a tip will still be appreciated. Often, the tips work in reverse with a free plate of fruit, a liqueur or brandy being routinely given to favoured customers. Taxi drivers will expect you to round up the bill by a Euro or two. Hotel housekeeping staff will be appreciative of a suitable tip if you have been well served through your stay (and it's a good way of getting rid of that pocket-full of small change you've acquired over your vacation!)

Toilets

There are virtually no public toilets on the Ionian Islands. Where the occasional facility is found, they are inevitably in poor condition, dirty and with the toilet seat missing. The use of a local bar or restaurant facility will normally be tolerated, even without a purchase being made. This is particularly the case at beaches. Disabled facilities are woefully inadequate other than in the larger hotels.

The «Turkish» type of toilet - where you place your feet on «marks» surrounding little more than a hole in the floor and have to have an incredible aim - is no longer encountered in the Ionian - except very, very occasionally. However, as elsewhere in Greece, you should not put paper or sanitary towels down the toilet as the pipes are extremely narrow and will rapidly block. A small basket or bin will be placed strategically nearby. Although initially this takes a little getting used to, in your own interest, use it! The free flowing sewage that is otherwise likely to greet you is even less desirable!

ionian
atoz

V

Vegetarians

There are only a few restaurants which cater specifically for vegetarians. Those who will eat fish are readily catered for. In other respects, your best bet lies with a selection of the starters routinely available from most Greek restaurants. Yoghurt dips, fried aubergines, mushrooms in cream sauce, "horta" - literally a spinach-like weed - served with fresh lemon and vinegar - these and many other mouth-watering platters are delicious. The ubiquitous Greek salad, "Houriatiki", cheese pies and spinach pies, stuffed peppers or tomatoes with savoury rice are all on the menu. Most restaurants will now have at least one or two vegetarian main courses on their menu - regrettably you may still only be offered the cheese omelette!

The best prospect for the vegetarian is often to self-cater. Check the standard of the cooking facilities available in your apartment though. Often, the cooker consists of but a couple of heating rings and a less than adequate selection of pans. If staying in a hotel, you would be advised to take only bed and breakfast arrangements. You will consistently be offered meat or, at best, chicken and fish otherwise.

Visas

Visas are not required for citizens of European Union nations. Passports are shown, but not stamped. Those from the USA, Australia, Canada etc., have their passport stamped - effectively acting as a holiday visa - and must normally complete a landing card at their first port or airport of entry. Such informal visas are normally valid three months.

W

Water

The water supply on the Ionian Islands is normally perfectly wholesome. However, as a commodity in relatively short supply, the provision is not always suitable for drinking. Hotel bedrooms tend to utilize drinkable water. However, just a change in water supply from that you're used to at home can affect your stomach. If you're at all sensitive in this way, use the bottled water available very cheaply from supermarkets. Watch out for the difference in price between certain brands. It can sometimes be significant. If you can't work out why your stomach is unsettled, try knocking off any ice added to your favourite drink!

Water Sports

There are water sports available on most resort beaches. Provision includes paragliding, water skiing, windsurfing, dinghy sailing, canoeing, pedaloes, jet skis and motor boats. Ensure that those who run the outlet are qualified and authorized to operate the facility. Also make sure you are always issued with life preservers, whatever sort of water sports you undertake.

Y

Yacht Service

There is an authorised port of entry on each island. A small number of marinas and, otherwise, quayside yacht services exist at various ports and harbours throughout the Ionian. Services routinely include refueling, fresh water, ice and local provisions. Less often, but still relatively frequently, you will come across, laundry, internet cafes, shower facilities and even marine repairs.

□ **a**
accommodation....................170
airports................................170

□ **b**
banks...................................172
bomba.................................172
buses...................................173

□ **c**
carrental.............................173
chemists..............................174
contraception.......................174
creditcards........................174
currency...............................174

□ **d**
dentists................................175
diarrhoea.............................175
disabledaccess.................175
diving...................................176
doctors................................176
duty**free**goods....................177

□ **e**
earth**tremors**.....................177
electricitysupply.................177
emergency**phone**numbers...177

□ **f**
ferries..................................178

□ **i**
island**hopping**....................179

□ **j**
jellyfish................................179

□ **m**
maps....................................179
medicalinsurance...............180
mosquitoes..........................180

□ **n**
naturism...............................181
newspapers.........................181

□ **o**
openinghours............181

□ **p**
petrolstation..............182
pharmacies...................182
police............................182
postalfacilities............183

□ **r**
rainfall...........................183
restaurants...................184
room**rates**..................185

□ **s**
safety**deposit**boxes...185
scorpions.....................185
seaside**perils**............185
sea**urchins**................186
sizes.............................186
snakes..........................186

□ **t**
taxis.............................187
telephones...................187
temperature.................188
timezone...................188
tipping..........................188
toilets...........................189

□ **v**
vegetarians..................189
visas............................190

□ **w**
water............................190
water**sports**...............190

□ **y**
yachtservice...............190